RECOLLECTIONS OF AN UNSUCCESSFUL SEAMAN

BY LEONARD NOAKE

EDITED BY
DAVID CREAMER

Whittles Publishing

Published by
Whittles Publishing Ltd.,
Dunbeath,
Caithness, KW6 6EG,
Scotland, UK

www.whittlespublishing.com

© 2018 David Creamer
reprinted with addendum 2019

ISBN 978-184995-393-1

Printed and bound in Great Britain by
Severn, Gloucester

CONTENTS

About the Book, the Author, and the Editor

The Book

The original manuscript is typed and liberally illustrated with detailed pen and ink drawings, exquisite watercolour sketches, black-and-white photographs, and the occasional picture postcard. The 235 numbered pages have been professionally bound in leather with the front cover inscribed in gold lettering with the title, *Recollections of an Unsuccessful Seaman*. For some obscure reason the author's name, George Leonard (Len) Noake, is not included.

The book was written in 1928–1929 whilst Len, who was terminally ill with tuberculosis, alternated between being nursed at his home in Southwick, Sussex, and the Swandean Isolation Hospital in Worthing, where he was to pass away at the age of 42 on 21 November 1929. It will never be known whether he had the satisfaction of seeing his completed work in book form, or whether it was bound after his death.

Len's wife, Mabel, was to outlive her husband by over 40 years until her death in 1970. Their daughter Anitra, the youngest of three children, discovered her father's book in the loft of the family home in Lewes, Sussex, whilst sorting through her late mother's possessions. Unbelievably, its existence had never been disclosed by Mabel who was, according to Anitra, a very private and unassuming lady who shared very few stories or memories of Len with their children.

The book suffered from water damage in 2001 when Anitra's home, also in Lewes, was flooded. The water-based paint used in many of the sketches ran, causing the colours to become smudged and blotched and the leather cover was irreparably damaged; over time, some pages have become faded and stained. The book was rebound in 2016 in a new leather cover. Thankfully, the manuscript itself remained legible, and some of the author's skilled artistic efforts, carefully reproduced using modern scanning and colour enhancing techniques, are unaffected. Their survival ensures that Len's work will be recognised as a true and unpretentious insight into life in the mercantile marine almost 90 years ago.

THE AUTHOR

George Leonard Noake, or Len, as his family and friends always called him, was born in Worcester on 25 September 1887. Little is known of his childhood; his father, Charles Noake, was a Lloyd's Bank inspector, and records show the family to be living in Birmingham when Len commenced his pre-sea training on board the nautical training establishment HMS *Conway* in February 1903.

On completion of his pre-sea training in July 1905, Len served an apprenticeship until 1908, but details, once again, are sparse. In the book he writes that he fell 40 feet from aloft during this period; on the basis of this statement, I have assumed that his early seagoing career was 'under sail', and that he fell from the rigging of a sailing vessel in which he was serving. He also mentions having visited South America prior to his voyage on a tanker in 1918. Since his detailed memoirs begin in 1908, and there is no record of him sailing to South America between 1908 and 1918, it can also be assumed that this earlier visit occurred during his three-year apprenticeship. The reason behind him choosing not to include this period in his recollections remains a frustrating mystery – it may have been that he hadn't kept a log for his early voyages, or perhaps he chose to ignore, or forgot, his first years at sea. Likewise, he chooses not to share details with the reader of his working on a farm in Devon between 1913 and 1915, or his courtship with Mabel prior to their wartime marriage in November 1916.

Len was clearly a lively but proud and responsible person, fond of a tipple, and blessed with a great self-belief that he would get by, though not necessarily prosper, in his chosen career. He was never out of work for too long despite the depression and hard times in the shipping industry. His financially disastrous ventures into farming and road haulage show him to have been a gullible yet hard-working and very determined individual, as does the writing of his recollections during a time when he quite clearly knew he was terminally ill.

As with all professions where the breadwinner has to spend lengthy periods away from his or her family, there is a fine line to be drawn between abandonment and support. In this respect, Len had difficult and heart-rending decisions to make, but his later work on coasting vessels, where he was closer to home, suggest his young family was never too far away from his immediate thoughts. It must be remembered that voyages of between six and 12 months were considered the norm in the period of his writing. His claims not to have been a 'Bolshie' ring a little untrue; his opinion of ship owners borders upon outright vilification. The last chapter in his book suggests he retained his fervent attitudes and militancy to the very end.

I would have considered it an immense honour to have met Len, my great-uncle. Editing and researching his memoirs has given me a very clear insight into his distinctive humour, and also an appreciation of his cheerful personality and resolute character. I find it hard to believe that he should be so demeaning as to think of himself as an 'unsuccessful seaman'.

THE EDITOR

Little did my mother realise that returning home sometime in the 1990s, after visiting her first cousin Anitra, with a leather-bound book written by my great-uncle would start a project that has kept me occupied, on and off, for many years. As a master mariner myself, I was fascinated by the book. Here was an unpublished account of seafaring life in the early 1900s that included enthralling stories of foreign ports, of being torpedoed during the First World War, and of the hardships and suffering experienced by the men of the mercantile marine during the worldwide shipping depression of the 1920s. I felt it almost my duty to make the book available to a readership far wider than our immediate family and friends. Over the next few months, I transcribed the entire manuscript, word for word, spelling mistake for spelling mistake, into a file in my computer, where it remained unopened but not completely forgotten for a considerable period of time.

In 2005, I belatedly made my acquaintance with Anitra and her own family in Lewes. During my visit, I sought Anitra's permission to try to publish her father's work. She was enthusiastic, delighted that someone else was appreciating and recognising her father's efforts. She insisted upon me taking the water-damaged book back home so that I would be able to work on it at my leisure. It was with a greatest sadness that I learnt of her passing in April 2007.

The original manuscript had little hope of being accepted for publication; political correctness and changes in the English language over nearly 90 years have rendered some of the original manuscript unprintable. I was reassured by publishers that by editing my great-uncle's work, I would not be detracting from his literary efforts, and that the original unpublished and unedited manuscript would remain in the family's possession as a priceless heirloom of sentimental value.

Editing and researching Len's fascinating recollections has not been easy. Every effort has been made to portray and reproduce the original manuscript as it was written, but in many instances it has been necessary to shuffle words and sentences to enable the story to flow in a more logical sequence. I will also admit to having used 'editor's licence' in making my own very occasional interpretation of what I think Len intended to write when some of his sentences were found to be totally confused or disjointed. It is for this reason that some original paragraphs and the final chapter, set out for easy identification, have been included within the manuscript to allow the reader to understand the author's style of writing. It is difficult to comprehend how someone so very ill and weak could sit behind a typewriter and, from memory and possibly a journal, write and illustrate a story of such compelling interest and detail.

My research into his career and the names of the ships in which he served would not have been possible without the Liverpool Maritime Museum, Southampton City Council Archives, and the Toronto University, which accepted responsibility for the safekeeping of our national maritime archives when, a few years ago, the British Government inexplicably decided to dispose of most of the country's seafaring records.

David Creamer, 2017

ACKNOWLEDGEMENTS

In memory of both my great uncle, George Leonard Noake (d.1929), who wrote this work in 1928/29, and also his daughter, Anitra (d.2007), who shared my desire to see her father's work published.

To all those at Whittles Publishing, who have made it possible for me to honour my promise to Anitra.

To my wife, Hilary, for enduring many hours of loneliness, to all those at Liverpool Maritime Museum, Southampton City Council and Toronto University for assisting me in my research a few years ago, and to Lindsay, the proprietor of Bookbane in north Wales, for painstakingly restoring the original manuscript and rebinding it in a new leather cover.

INTRODUCTION

Man that is born of woman has but a short time to live,
He comes in like a maintops staysail, and goes out like a flying jib.

R. F. W. Rees, *The Second Mate*[i]

Here I am, admitted to a public sanatorium and hospital with all the symptoms of an excessive intake of liquid refreshments and with consumption of the lungs. This is my reward for spending the last 20 years being one of those misguided persons going down to the sea in ships to occupy their 'labahs' upon the great 'watahs'.

This Swandean Hospital[ii] in Worthing for incurable consumptives is about as cheerful as the mouth of the Elbe in a north-east gale on a winter's night. I have lain in bed for months not feeling very well; they have been expecting me to die for some time, but one cannot keep all one's appointments, not to time anyway. I feel sorry for some of the poor chaps here; those who are not actually dying seem, for the most part, to be far too ill to have a good yarn. I should have died a long time ago, several times in fact. Whilst sailing as an apprentice I fell 40 feet from aloft, and followed this up with rheumatic fever and scurvy. When I left the West African trade, a kindly German doctor gave me just 12 months to live. Then there was the ship I failed to join, which was lost with all hands, and the big tramp steamer that disappeared the voyage after I had been paid off. I also came very close to bleeding to death from head injuries after being attacked by some robbers in a lonely part of the docks in a French port. Yes, I am sure you will be sorry for me when you learn that I have been a great sufferer from bad heads, despite them generally occurring after either imbibing too much internal liniment or incurring severe financial cramp.

They seem woefully behind the times in this public sanatorium and hospital, with the doctors appearing to know no more than I do about treating tuberculosis. The young nurses don't like being told they couldn't cure a kipper, never mind a patient, and yet the old saying goes that all the nice girls love a sailor! There is no modern apparatus, no X-rays, artificial sunrays, or any other rays for that matter. They do have an excellent stock of fresh air, a bottle of cough mixture, and a flask of cascara sagrada, but that just about sums up their stock in trade. Instead of giving oxygen to a man on his last gasp, they should give him Sanatogen[iii] much earlier and then the deaths might be fewer. You hear far too much of this 'fresh air' business; no one could get much more of it than I have by sailing across the North Sea for a couple of years, but it hasn't done me any good.

I am now able to sit on a deckchair on the lawn and keep a lookout on the high fence that shuts us off very completely from the outside world. I can walk up and down the narrow strip of grass as if it were an imaginary ship's bridge and even talk to an imaginary helmsman, but I am tired of these occupations. I've read every book in the place, even *The Constant Nymph*[iv] which shows just how desperate one can become. I have found scientific books about atoms and electrons to be all very wonderful, but they're only for the improvement of trade or machine and not for us humans. The nearest approach to a cure for this complaint is all about money and being able to take advantage of what it will buy rather than science. I recently paid nine pence for a book entitled *How to Cure Tuberculosis*, but to no real benefit other than to the bookseller's pocket.

I've also had better food for 14 shillings a week in a coasting steamer than I've had in this place. I am sure you have seen those Indian fakir fellows, or photographs of them. We all appear exactly the same, just skin and bones. My legs look like an optical illusion with my thighs no thicker than an ordinary man's forearm, and as for my calves! For most of the patients, however, these sanatoriums are a godsend and they are infinitely better off in hospital than they would be in their own homes. It just needs someone in high authority to run around with a flannel hammer and to tap the brains of those in charge to wake them up before they get into a groove.

There is no amusement provided for the patients unless the parson's weekly visits should count, but I'm sure they're not intended as such! He is quite a nice man the parson, but another sufferer. He suffers from the truly ghastly complaint of speaking with a very parsonical voice, even in ordinary conversation: 'My poor fellow, you are not looking yourself today.' That cheers me up no end until I reach for the mirror. And then he continues, 'I will now read to you from the *Scriptyahs*,' which reminds me of George, a steward aboard a little coasting boat in which I was sailing as chief mate. George also had a parsonical voice; he would come creeping into my cabin the morning after the night before with the greeting 'blessed are the weak for they shall be comforted', before sharing the glass of whisky or bottle of beer he had brought with him as a means of providing the further comfort we both sought.

As I've said before, there is nothing to do in the hospital to keep one amused. Needlework on cushion covers doesn't appeal to me, and I lose my wool mending my socks. I'll have to fall back on my old logbook and live in the past. A rolling stone may not collect much moss, but it can collect an awful lot of memories. After months of monotony one feels one simply must break out somehow, so I am going to break out by writing my recollections, even if they should be as rambling as I have been these past few months. The only really sensible thing I can remember doing is getting married,ᵛ although I suppose you will say the next sensible thing will be my getting buried. I can give no details about that for the moment; medical opinion suggests it won't be too long.

Recalling my life will not be easy, but there will be one or two good features in the book at least!

This beautiful art plate of the author comes free with the book.

Yours truly,
The unsuccessful seaman

1 ⚓ A Voyage to Africa

What the Admiralty Sailing Directions say about the West Coast of Africa.

From ten o'clock in the morning till
five in the evening a white man is seldom
seen abroad; at the latter hour, the racecourse and the premenade on the battery are
frequented by equestrians and pedestrians;
and, perhaps, no circumstance that strikes
the attention of a stranger, makes so strong an
impression on his mind as the general expression
he observes of languor and debility in the looks of
every individual he meets of European birth (with
perhaps two or three exceptions) in the colony. The young and old,
the acclimated even as they are deemed, who have had their seasoning,
either in one fever, or the periodical return of that malady, and have
survived these attacks, show plainly enough the baneful influence of the
climate, which leaves the future without vivacity, and frame without
vigour, and the whole constitution apparently deficient in vitality.

"The English oil-traders never live on shore. Vast hulks of East
Indiamen, once floating palaces or stores, are the houses of the agents;
while trading vessels sometimes remain three years in a river, their
decks covered with a thatched roof. These ship-villages are governed
by a council of captains, who punish thieves and mutineers, and act as
a Court of Arbitration, there being a power of appeal to the Consul of
Fernando Po, who visits the rivers from time to time in a man-of-war.
Half a century ago the delta was merely a slave-exporting land; and the
palm oil traffic is quite of recent date. In 1808 our imports of the oil
did not exceed 200 tons a year; at present they amount to about 50,000
tons. In this Delta of the Niger, the refuge of reckless and despairing
men, Death, as if sure of its victims, throws off the mask. Once enter
that gloomy land, and the impression can never be effaced. The rivers

filthy as sewers; the slimy mud stinking in the sun; the loathsome crocodiles lying prone upon it, and showing their white bellies as they sullenly plunge into the stream; the foaming, shark-haunted bars; the hideous aspect of the people, whose bodies are usually covered with sores; the traders with their corpse-like faces – all this can be remembered, but cannot be described. The tribes which occupy the lower regions of these rivers monopolise the inland trade, and their chiefs acquire considerable wealth."

"Here a European must look after himself; for the inhabitants are so subtilly mischievous, that you will be betrayed before you are aware; and they are so barbarously cruel, that the parents sell their children, and the husband his wife, one brother and sister the other; and, in decency and order, are scarecely a degree above the beasts."

This description was written in the seventeenth century, and we do not find the inhabitants have improved since that time. (1890)

Among the predisposing causes of sickness, one of the most frequent is the dread and prostration of spirits that pervades almost every class of people on their first visit to this unhealthy coast. The unremitting fatality of the diseases, united with the depressing influences of climate, have certainly gained for this part of the globe, an unenviable notoriety, which time can never dissipate. Notwithstanding the array of fearful drawbacks, individuals may reside in the majority of these regions, unimpaired in health and constitution, for a considerable number of years, by proper care and attention to hygiene considerations, by cheerfulness and confidence relative to future results, regularity and a tropical adaptation of diet, by a determination to resist hypochondriacal forebodings, or despondent impressions, by the appropriate employment of time in judicious mental and physical labour or recreations.

In those pre-war days from 1908 to 1913, when trade grew and changed enormously, a voyage from the Continent to West Africa was said to be one of the toughest in the mercantile marine. In the years I mention, there were no trade union secretaries opening harbours, for there were no harbours to speak of on that vast stretch of coastline, and there were no native kings emptying their bottles of gin on the beach to set a good example for their subjects!

There was hardly a coastal village from Dakar to the Congo that wasn't visited by the company's vessels. I was on all the different runs at one time or another – the creeks, the oil rivers, and the Congo. We sailed from Hamburg to the slimy and shark-infested Niger creeks, leaving a trail of trade gin at every little out-of-the-way factory (as these trading stations were called) from Sierra Leone to the Cameroons, and then down the fever-reeking Gabon and Muni rivers to load mahogany and other wood for the return voyage to Hamburg. Unlike the mail boats from England, we had none of the pleasures of orchestras, French menus, ships' doctors, or other luxuries. On these steamers, we just made do with rum, bully beef, and pyjamas instead.

The steamship SS *Mango*, in which I sailed as second mate, was an old rattletrap engaged in the West African trade. In the two years I was on board she was commanded by five different masters: one too shaky to hold a sextant, one a card fiend who would play patience going through the surf, two who were really quite mad, and the last a teetotaller. As the second officer, I was reckoned to be a little crazy, but the chief officers were considerably worse. One took drugs and another consumed trade gin, or 'methylated' as it is known, a practice not tolerated even on this coast.

Sailing from Hamburg in the SS *Mango* is quite an experience. With many thousands of green cases of gin, a few additional trade goods loaded in her rusty interior, the lower bridge piled high with potatoes and other items for the captain's private trade, and with a dozen dogs to be sold down the coast kennelled in the forecastle, the *Mango* swirls past the gay night haunts of St. Pauli,[i] down into the dreary lower reaches of the Elbe, and out into the teeth of a howling north-westerly gale. The old packet wallows, creaks, and groans under protest at her top speed of about seven knots through the bad weather and the nasty seas in the English Channel before she can enter the Bay of Biscay.

The deck cargo of heavy oil drums breaks loose from its lashings off Dover and by midnight what remains of the third mate, who had left the bridge to see what was wrong, has to be carried back to his cabin located in the officers' accommodation under the poop. To cross the slippery decks that are continuously awash from the heavy seas with dry clothes in one hand and clutching the lifeline in the other is indeed a feat, not one of dry feet though. The third officer's body is landed ashore at Plymouth. We lie at anchor for a couple of days windbound before setting off into the worst gale I had ever seen in the Bay of Biscay. With wicked grey-green curling monsters rearing high above the forecastle head, she dips down into the appalling deep troughs between the rollers, regular 'Cape Horners' I would call them, but more dangerously steep. For three days she lies with her nose to the shrieking wind, her cargo derricks swinging perilously and with the engines broken down. The skipper really thought the old tub was doomed and finished when the first mate was injured. By instinct, physique, brain, and mind, I am the conventional 'office' man if ever there was one, never as happy as when doing the accounts, manifests, and ship's business. I find myself beginning to dislike the sea life, but it is too late now.

She didn't go down though and hasn't done yet as far as I know. A few years ago I saw her name on a sale board in a Fenchurch Street office: 'The fine full powered steamer *Mango*.' Evidently there are advantages in not telling the whole truth when it comes to advertising!

The skipper dashes me a bottle of champagne when we get her on a southerly course once more. After six-hour watches on that sodden lurching bridge and messing about with the sea anchor and oil bags in between, one needs a tonic. The German crew are steady and good workers, but they aren't at their best in those conditions. After crossing the Bay, we arrive off Las Palmas where we lie at anchor on her rusty cable for a few hours before heading south to meander along the monotonous sandy coastline of Gambia and the swampy peninsula of Sierra Leone.

For people who are easily influenced, there is a great deal of romance attached to this part of the world. British philanthropists founded the colony of Sierra Leone in 1787 with 400 repatriated slaves and 40 European prostitutes. Most of them died from disease and fighting the local tribes, but obviously nature took its course because look at the number of people in the colony now. Personally I never want to see the confounded country again.

At Sierra Leone, 60 'Kroo'[ii] boys are shipped as stevedores to discharge the vessel's cargo along the coast and to load her up with the logged wood exports. No accommodation is provided for them on board so they sleep on the iron decks. They work from early morning to nightfall and live on a diet of salt meat and rotten fish. The distinguishing sign of the tribe is the blue tattoo mark on their foreheads. Being the most intelligent on the coast, there are some good sailors in their midst. The headman is in sole charge of the crowd and in cases of insubordination or arguments amongst them, the offender is lashed to the rigging and soundly flogged.

From Monrovia, where the head customs official was caught going ashore with the captain's cat under his very much gold braided uniform coat, we progress slowly down the Grain, Windward, Ivory, and Gold coasts,[iii] landing trade gin and cotton goods onto the sandy beaches where the Atlantic rollers ceaselessly thunder. Since the war, trade with the Gold Coast has increased tremendously, probably because it is the richest country in the world for its size, exporting half the world's cocoa supply, a quarter of the manganese ore, and large quantities of palm oil, gold, diamonds, and bananas. In what was until quite recently 'Darkest Africa', 500 new motor car licences were issued in 1928 in the city of Kumasi.

With a harbour on the Gold Coast becoming imperative, Sir Robert McAlpine commenced work in 1921 building the port of Takoradi, a few miles southwest of Sekondi. The harbour is some 200 acres in extent and cost around £4 million to build, but at the time of writing, every ton of cargo is landed on the palm-fringed beaches by means of surf boats.

Here and there we pick up native deck passengers including many young dusky belles. They flaunt their high-heeled French shoes and open work silk stockings and are generally accompanied by half-naked black servants and howling babies. They always carry with them various household effects including that useful ceramic article of toilet-ware often found beneath the bed.

In the early morning mist the vessel anchors as near to the roaring surf edge as she can safely lie. With the rattle of her cable announcing our arrival, the surf boats leave the shore manned by half-naked boat boys paddling as a man to a fantastic chant. I must say it is as well to be on good terms with these boat boys as a capsized boat is a frequent occurrence. Aboard the *Mango*, the 'mammy chair', a box-like contrivance for landing passengers, is slung overside from the derrick head and filled with a laughing, fighting swarm of natives with their umbrellas, babies, pots and pans, looking glasses, poultry, and what not. The chair is swung clear of the rolling decks, the winch rattles, and they are deposited pell-mell into the heaving surf boat far beneath.

The first boat takes the third officer ashore, an experience that on a bad day he will never forget. From the steamer, it doesn't look so alarming, but once in the boat, the crested white foaming walls ahead rapidly grow in dimensions. At a signal from the headman positioned at the big steering oar aft, the paddles cease for a moment. Waiting for a great green-capped roller to tower astern, he gives a blood-curdling yell and the paddles furiously stab the water. The heavily laden boat swinging high onto the breaking crest of the wave is propelled at tremendous speed into the safety of the shallow water, where a moment later a crewman will carry ashore the boat's passengers.

The third officer's duties are to wander around the beach, superintend the discharging and loading of the boats, and collect liquid refreshment and the signed bills of lading[iv] from the various factories. Meanwhile, on the steamer, the first and second officers tally the cargo as it comes from the hold and then see it safely into the waiting surf boats.

Occasionally the surf gets too heavy for the boats to return to the ship, leaving the third officer stranded on the beach. This is no great hardship, for the hospitality ashore is generally good and wet. I was once hosted by a royal who was dressed in decrepit check trousers and a topper a size too large. He was a most hospitable old chap who gave me a warm bottle of lager and asked which of his three daughters I would like to entertain me for the evening.

In recent years, the ship's officer's duties have changed and they no longer do this kind of work. They have also lost the traditional perk of collecting 'excessive luggage' fees from the native passengers in exchange for a worthless piece of paper purporting to be the company's receipt, a practice from which they innocently made a few extra shillings and, in my opinion, quite deservedly so.

It is hard work along this coast for the ship's officer. The steamer can often call in at three ports in one day between the early morning and sunset. In addition to working in the day, the second officer keeps his navigational watch from midnight until 4 a.m. on the bridge whilst the vessel cruises along the coast to arrive off the next village by daylight. The middle watch at night can be four long sleepy hours. Although there is little sea traffic, the thunderstorms can be terrific. Sometimes glowing balls of fire seem to rest upon the mastheads and it is often possible to read on the bridge by the light of the continuous vivid lightning. It is said to be the most luminous part of the Atlantic Ocean with the whole sea surface appearing as if it were a sheet of liquid fire with the bow wave throwing a sickly glare through the broken water. The whole experience can be particularly unnerving and distinctly unpleasant for the novice watchkeeper alone on the bridge. In the wet seasons, the nights are dark and gloomy with a strong breeze and not a solitary star to be seen. The second officer must also superintend the lowering of the ten-ton steam launch that is used for towing the boats to the edge of the surf. When the ship is rolling heavily, this can be very dangerous work.

The voyage continues into the Bight of Benin, heading towards the dreary and depressing town of Forçados before carrying on up the narrow and tortuous mangrove creeks to Wari, Benin, Sapele, and Abonnema. The creeks are evil smelling and alligator infested, with screaming parrots flying overhead and inquisitive monkeys peering out from the mangrove branches. Hanging from some of the branches an old kettle or bucket can be occasionally spotted; they have been hung there as symbols of the queer native 'Ju-Ju', or witchcraft, and will have their very own mysterious meanings.

Some of the carved ebony 'Ju-Jus' for sale in England are from Birmingham. In 1928, 'Ju-Jus' became all the rage in the drawing rooms of Paris and London. Artists produced them and call it 'Exotic Art', but whilst they carved some of the female shape, modesty prevented them from including all of it.

The water is deep yet in places the vessel brushes aside the mangrove trees growing from the riverbanks. The native pilots have a good memory for the twists and turns in the channel despite there being very many blind creeks. A wrinkled old man clad only in a broken bowler and a smile gives us a wave as he fishes from a frail dugout. It never was a health resort around here, but for the old timers it must have been pure hell.

A local magnate goes swiftly past in his big canoe, the paddles manned by his numerous wives and with the chief himself sitting aft drinking his gin under the shade of a large green umbrella. In these parts, although native wives only clean and do other light work, they will probably have less to do than in many houses back at home and their lives will be that much easier than the majority of the poor women I have met in merry England, much to the benefit of their figures:

> Ladies, if you want that slim and upright figure, then copy these native women. A few simple exercises walking in a state of nature through some wood with a soft article such as a few pounds of rubber on your heads and, if you have babies, these can be lashed on your back whilst you exercise. This will do the trick.

Wherever a horrible climate and good business profits combine, the Scots make the best colonists. Anyone who can survive purely on porridge in the western highlands of Scotland in winter can stand anything in this world and maybe even the next. Macgregor Laird[v] was reportedly one of the first of many intrepid explorers to enter the almost-impenetrable Niger Delta. Although the climate was frightful and the natives about as safe as a tiger with the toothache, he managed to reach the fat old local king and exchange a double of the real stuff and a spare kilt for a boatload of ivory. A fair exchange when profits are concerned!

Nigeria is not a country in which to linger and is of absolutely no use at all to the prohibitionist. Brigadier General Frank P. Crozier[vi] CB, CMG, DSO, writing in the *Sunday Express*, said: 'the drink was appalling when he was in Nigeria'. When I visited that salubrious country, the drink was whisky and there was plenty of it.

When we round Cape Formosa the climate becomes most depressing. This coastline is more or less one huge interminable swamp and, without exception, the most deadly part of the whole west coast of Africa. We anchor in the Rio del Rey under the shadow of mighty volcanic mountains before heading south to the little rocky islet of Fernando Poo that was named after one of the three navigators who discovered it and two other islands. Cameroon is wild. The natives are enthusiastic headhunters and skull worshippers and members of the hemp smoker's fraternity; not nice people at all.

We reach the Gabon River in the rainy season and it pours down continuously; a musty-smelling white mist shrouds the mangrove swamps. The vast country of Cameroon lies to the north and the French Congo to the south. This is a sad, dismal, and fever-stricken coast that has no attractions apart from the opportunity for an individual to make a bit of money, but even that will be done away with.

Within 24 hours of our arrival our second engineer dies of malaria fever whilst the third and fourth engineers and I suffer from frequent attacks. It is surprising the difference in effect a stiff dose of the fever could have between a big hearty German such as our fourth engineer, who is left a miserable wreck, and a skinny individual like myself who experiences little or no change. The chief officer, whose brain is affected, has to remain in a hospital further up the coast, leaving me to act in his place. We hope to call for him on the way back. The natives are by no means immune from the fever, and I find myself having to give medicine to the Kroo boys as and when required, which is frequently. They relish black draught mixed with Epsom salts and sip castor oil as if it were liquor. There are many complaints requiring attention: yaws, which covers the body with running sores; elephantiasis; malaria; and syphilis.

The ship lies at anchor for some three weeks at the entrance to the Gabon River, taking on board the rafts of logs floated down from up country. The third officer tows the rafts alongside the steamer with the steam launch, but sometimes the grass rope lashings part and a dozen or so logs escape in all directions in the eddying current, giving the third officer the job of rounding them up.

Hoisting logs, which can weigh anything from four tons to eight tons, on our shaky derricks is dangerous work in the extreme. With the great baulk swinging from bulwark to bulwark with the roll of the ship, the winch boy has to wait for his chance to lower it with a run into the hold below. Sometimes the derrick or wire rope will carry away and should there be a native underneath when the log comes crashing down onto the deck, there is a nasty mess. The officer must nail a tin tally onto the log and record its number in a book before climbing into the hold below to superintend its stowage. This is no easy matter with logs from 20 to 50 feet long, and often it becomes like a giant jigsaw puzzle to load the full cargo.

And all the time it rains! Getting wet, externally of course, and staying wet in this unhealthy and fever-ridden climate is to court disaster. With a deck-load of logs aft and some space left to fill up homeward bound, the *Mango* has, at long last, loaded most of her cargo.

Whilst loading the logs we bought an alligator in the hopes of selling it for a good profit in Hamburg. Unfortunately, the beast had other ideas, and after it had escaped and chased the cook, we helped it over the side. We still have a selection of melancholy-looking monkeys and some shrieking parrots that we plan to sell to animal dealers on the Continent.

We leave the Gabon River and steam across the Bight of Benin towards Cape Palmas off Liberia, crossing the point on the equator at the Greenwich Meridian where both the latitude and longitude read nothing at all. Had we more cargo space, we would stop off at other ports on the homeward passage to pick up a few of the great whitewashed puncheons of palm oil, or some sacks of kernels or cocoa, or some barrels of stinking raw rubber, or even some dingy ivory tusks.

It is refreshing to all on board to get the good salt breeze again, but a dangerous time for the fever patients. It is said the soundings of the ocean bottom from West Africa to Las Palmas will only show a trail of human bones and empty bottles. We hear of a vessel that was rendered helpless two days after leaving Dakar, in Senegal, when the entire crew was struck down with malaria fever. It is not a pleasant business, this malaria fever.

We call in to the Sierra Leone River to take bunkers and to land the Kroo boys, who are paid off after receiving their present of a barrel of rotten salt meat and a cask of rum between them. A few days after leaving Sierra Leone we anchor off Madeira to load wine. The cargo is delivered to the ship in lighters with the casks ranging from huge hogsheads to the tiniest of barrels. With the arrival of the bumboat man, the chief mate becomes occupied with his own private business; in a very short time the crew are as drunk as owls and the carpenter's tally of the wine casks being loaded closely resembles Egyptian hieroglyphics. The captain returns on board with the last lighter. I'm not much of a wine drinker myself and being quite sober, I find myself being very bad tempered at having to steer the ship alone in the first watch after sailing from the island.

After a 10,000-mile voyage, the ship arrives in Hamburg to discharge her cargo. Long before the vessel is made fast, the local wine and spirit merchant is on board selling beer for a penny a bottle and a good Scotch whisky for two shillings and sixpence per bottle. We go ashore later, some in search of beauty and some in search of booze. Some are looking for both, but they needed to look no further than St. Pauli, a suburb of Hamburg that has been described as *the* resort for sailors and is, without doubt, the most gay or some might even call it the most wicked of all the continental ports, bar none.

St. Pauli is the centre of Hamburg's underworld. The glittering open-all-night cafes are filled with hundreds of women of all ages, mostly pretty and some quite beautiful, but where one and all are members of the oldest profession in the world. Fine string orchestras play real music throughout the night; under one of the cafes is a barber's shop splendidly fitted out with soft layback chairs for a livening head massage, and bathrooms where you can take a bath, or even a jolt of dope should you feel so inclined. London nightclubs are a miserable joke when compared with those of St. Pauli.

The German women who ply their trade in this quarter are unusual in that they appear most 'homelike' and clean, a trait not to be found elsewhere. Imagine being in the middle of your 'early morning' lobster supper, sober yet having had a few drinks, when your girl companion invites you round to visit her flat in the evening so she can do any mending that needs to be done, or darn any socks that need to be darned. And she means it as well! I hear that these women make very good wives and that most of them are saving up to get married.

A luxuriously upholstered Chinese café is the meeting place for the pick of the younger girls who have come from all over the world. Here you can see a dainty Brazilian lady dressed in the latest Paris fashion, dancing with a placid and dapper Chinese man. It is sad but true that the young and attractive ladies have not yet realised that when age overtakes them, the café will no longer welcome them. The oldest profession is a tough old business.

When you walk the streets during the early hours of the morning, you will see another and more terrible side to the nightlife that is no different to any other city, but probably more pronounced here. You will be gently and politely accosted by dozens of women who have been sheltering in some dark doorway from the bitter midwinter wind that is far colder than in England. There is no warmth in their imitation furs and thin stockings; ask one into a small café for an icebreaker, or hot grog as you may know it, and she will show you hands that are blue with cold without any gloves and her knees will be like ice, yet they must keep at it. I can hardly write here what I should like to say, but the position of some of these women is very wretched to say the least. Their fortitude and bodily strength amazes me.

Hamburg is the city where most of our ill-gotten gains from the native deck passengers' 'excessive luggage' fees changed hands and for a short time our voyage to the 'coast' was completely forgotten. You'll probably be thinking I'm a nice old rogue, but the truth of the matter is that even when I was that much younger my interest in Bacchus was far greater than Venus. A pity you might say, but there it is!

2   THE HORSE TRANSPORT

It is 1915 and we are at war with Germany. The British Transport ship is berthed in Cardiff docks in the pouring rain, lying close to the roaring coal hoists and the piles of pit props stacked on the quayside. The 100 or so horse tenders, or stablehands as we might call them, roughly in equal numbers of white and black men, come from the slums of New York, Chicago, and San Francisco, and they are making merry whilst they can for we will be sailing in the morning. They look after the horses we are shipping from the States and return on the westbound trip as passengers. All night long they sing, fight, and curse. Two drunken Negroes armed with razors slash vaguely at each other amidst the debris of beer cases looted from the steward's store. The place stinks like a cesspool and their quarters are a complete shambles into which the dock police are not anxious to intrude.

Should this vessel be sunk by a torpedo or a mine, some of those on board will have their first bath for years, and probably their last. I hear these horse tenders are apt to be in a hurry to get to the boats, and we are very overcrowded. During the voyage across the Atlantic, a couple of drug addicts run short of supplies and end their misery by jumping over the side; otherwise, the two foremen manage to keep reasonable order. Tough merchants, these horse tender foremen. Sam, a professional hobo, has tramped England as well as the States and he has a grievance. He worked for a Herefordshire farmer, the meanest in the whole of Europe, who paid him only 12 shillings for a whole week's hard work. The other foreman, who has been a sailor on a windjammer and a fisherman on the Great Banks, is quite a good fellow despite having spent some time in jail.

There is not a British seaman amongst our crew with the exception of the baker and the officers' steward. We have Swedes, Greeks, Italians, a Mexican, a Malay, and the Turkish Empire is also represented; the bosun is a wizened old Maltese man and the bosun's mate is a Russian Jew.

On arrival at Newport News, Virginia, the ship is warped under the coal tips ready for bunkering. Just outside the town 3,000 horses from all over the States and as far as Mexico have been collected together in big corrals at Buckroe Beach.[i] For days these poor creatures have been shut up in the sweltering heat of railroad cars; many died even in the 'cool' of the evening when the temperature remained over 90°F at midnight. The horses are brought down in fours to the quayside sheds where they are given a rest overnight before being hustled on board in the cooler early morning hours. The animals are of all shapes and sizes and vary from the big raw-boned Texas mustang that is sweating and kicking like fury to the docile old animal from some far away Kentucky farm that ambles patiently up the gangway. The Negro horse-handlers are very skilled and succeed in getting 700 horses plus all their fodder and utensils on board for a voyage to England in only three hours. Packed from stem to stern with horseflesh, the whining electric fans make little difference to the heat and stench below decks; the lucky ones are the animals and their tenders in the fresh air of the upper deck.

Our short stay in Virginia is not without incident. The assistant vet, a German living in Boston, aired his views on the war too freely and has been kicked ashore to find other work. There has also been trouble amongst the culinary staff. The horse tender's cook, a fat oily Indian, insulted the Turkish ship's cook and a fight ensued. Strong words passed before knives appeared and a fireman was stabbed when trying to separate them. A warrant was taken out for the Indian's arrest, but he was nowhere to be found. Later in the evening, and much to everyone's surprise, he appeared outside the chief officer's cabin door and asked permission to go ashore for the evening to see his girlfriend. In the meantime, the Turk abandoned his job and 'jumped ship', never to be seen again. With time being too short to hire a replacement cook, the warrant was cancelled and the Indian promoted to being the ship's chef. It's a poor knife that doesn't do anyone any good!

We are soon back at sea; on the second day out, I'm leaning over the bridge rail enjoying the cool breeze when I see a row of heads pop out of the horseboxes on deck. The animals also appear to be revelling in the fresh air until it dawns on me that the wreath of smoke curling up from the bows shouldn't be there at all. A fire on a packed horse transport would be ghastly. We are lucky that this one is confined to the bosun's store and is promptly extinguished; on the other side of the bulkhead and just a few feet away is hay, oats, and straw for 700 horses for three weeks.

In the two voyages we made across the Atlantic, we lost only four out of the 1,400 horses we transported, which I believe was a record. The Canadian vet had every right to feel proud and was always boasting 'that there were no flies on him'; unfortunately that didn't stop the flies from landing on everyone else on board!

As we near the danger zone of the Western Approaches, the lifeboats are swung out and their launching crews mustered. My lot consists of two wireless operators, the baker, a Swede, two Greeks and three Negro horse tenders from the southern states. The bridge is barricaded round with bales of hay to protect the steering position in case of shellfire. The horses are restless and continuously neigh as they scent the approaching land. The amount of good manure being dumped overboard during the passage worried me. If only I could have had that manure a little later in my career when I went ashore to take up farming!

No sooner are we safely anchored off Avonmouth than we're ordered back out to sea to sail round to Liverpool. The German submarines are very active in the Irish Sea and many good ships, like the White Star liner *Arabic II*, [ii] and much war material have been lost in this way. The alarm is raised one morning when we spot twin periscopes ahead; fortunately they prove to be harmless, but I don't suppose the back legs of a dead horse have ever caused such a stir before!

3   A Trip to Canada

The horses are discharged onto the Liverpool landing stage and we sail for Canada almost at once, taking with us those of the horse tenders who aren't in gaol. Nine days later, after an uneventful crossing of the Atlantic, we arrive for bunker coal at Sydney, a pretty little harbour surrounded by pine forests on Cape Breton Island which lies to the south of Newfoundland. The town is reported to be 'dry' until we find some 'wet' in the first store we enter. Being good sailors and ambassadors, we always observe the customs of the country we are visiting!

We sail up the St. Lawrence River and berth in Montreal under a 300-foot grain elevator that looks like a large packing case affair. As soon as the ship is moored, a gang of men commences breaking up the horse pens whilst the horse tenders are driven away in motor lorries, under the surveillance of the police, to the railway station. These men live and play hard; despite it being November and getting cold here, many are poorly dressed, some walk in bare feet, and most of them carry not a single item of luggage, which does, admittedly, have its advantages when travelling.

A ship can arrive in Montreal in the morning and by night have her nose turned eastward towards the sea with 300,000 bushels[i] of grain in her holds. Canada is one of the great granaries of the world, but I can't say I like Montreal; it's too cold in November and the whisky is not to my taste. I find the Gaiety Music Hall[ii] as warm a spot as any in that city.

We load 3,500 tons of oats and 1,000 tons of hay before setting off for the 800-mile journey down the mighty and swift-flowing river to reach the 'blue water' of the open sea. The St. Lawrence River has a certain cold grandeur in the autumn season. We keep close along the southern shore, steaming past the clumsy square-sailed timber crafts plying their local trade between the grassy islands. In the distance we can see little farm houses with canvas covered ricks, and the low and level plains broken only by the occasional rocky hill, as if they were boulders intruding upon a freshly mowed lawn.

At Sorel, the river widens into a great lake – shallow, unprotected, and windswept – with a deep hidden waterway cut into the solid clay through which the ocean traffic can pass. Beyond the lake on the northern shore, the foothills grow higher and turn purple in the fading daylight. The sun slowly sets in a blood red sky, painting the vast river a soft amber below the deepening blue of the evening sky, and then…the steering gear fails and the vessel runs ashore on the rocks at a particularly nasty bend in the river. Fortunately she can be backed off, and then we scurry off downstream with the current behind us towards Quebec.

The engines refuse to go astern when we try to stop off at Quebec. The ship is swept some miles downriver before she can be brought up, and all the time she is taking in water fast. Without further delay, tugs are summoned and we are towed back upriver and the cargo rapidly discharged. In the dry dock, the ship's bottom is repaired and returned to a temporarily seaworthy condition at a cost of some £4,000.

I find Quebec to be a tranquil city, but as cold and hard as a diamond on a snow bank; a city where miracles are enacted daily in the way the little horse cabs slither down the steep icy streets in safety. From the chateau on the heights there is a fine view looking over Orleans Island and down the amphitheatre of the lower St. Lawrence. Six miles below the city are the Montmorency Falls,[iii] one of the finest water cascades in eastern Canada, made all the better by the café at the top of the falls that sells hard drinks.

After leaving the dry dock in a genuine blizzard, with the snow and wind making it impossible to see more than a few yards ahead, the ship drags her anchors and nearly goes ashore again. The cargo is loaded back on board and we sail off down the river steaming under the giant suspension bridge,[iv] the largest of its kind in the world. The serenity of this mighty stream seems to be absorbed by the many contented-looking little towns nestling near the river banks; the black pine woods outlined against the snow gives the country that frosted Christmas card appearance. At Father Point, which is practically at the entrance to the St. Lawrence River and the scene of the *Empress* disaster,[v] thin ice is beginning to form on the water and there is a green steely look about the distant mountains. It is high time the vessel is out of it.

I don't want to see eastern Canada again, but unfortunately my next voyage leads to my return, and the second glimpse is worse than the first. For all those

voyage from Gibraltar through the Mediterranean is made without showing our navigation lights and with our portholes darkened. We arrive off the low-lying coastline 16 days after sailing from Le Havre. The ship is conducted through the breakwaters and into the harbour by a pompous Egyptian pilot carrying a childish telescope and wearing yellow gloves and a red fez.

The teeming harbour is a picture of life, colour, and bustle, with launches rushing about, old sailing craft lying peacefully at anchor under the lee of the boulder breakwater, and huge troopships landing Australian soldiers. A large hospital ship, snow white except for the broad green band on her hull, glides smoothly through the harbour entrance on her way out to sea; at night she will be a blaze of green lights from stem to stern with a big red illuminated cross amidships.

The Mediterranean has never before seen such a variety of ships. There is a fleet of North Sea trawlers engaged in minesweeping; a continuous procession of giant liners, tramps, colliers and tugboats that have puffed up the Thames and the Clyde; and south coast pleasure steamers that will probably never again take sweethearts for a sixpenny trip in the moonlight to view the shipping in the Channel.

After our cargo of flour has been discharged, the ship is moved to the anchorage abreast of the famous old yacht the *Sunbeam*[i] to await further orders. One of those sheik-like fellows, who ply the harbour by the score in their fast sailing craft, will put us ashore for a shilling, but the curse of Allah will be upon us should we choose to ignore his demands for more money. The customs gate at the landing pier is lined with money changers pestering for business; immediately outside in the street one is surrounded by a yelling hoard of loafers, hawkers of postcards decent and indecent, hotel runners, curio sellers, cabmen, guides, beggars, and touts for whatever takes your fancy. You must push through and walk on for they will not follow for more than a quarter of a mile, and by then their prices are coming down with every step you take.

One persistent old cabman refuses to give up:

> "See Alexandria, Captain, Pompey's Pillar,[ii] the Catacombs,[iii] Kiedive Gardens,[iv] very nice place, Captain." His fare has now come down from ten shillings to three shillings each. "You no like Pompey's Pillar, Captain? No Sir, alright Sir. Very good, Captain, I know a nice pub, Sir! Plenty girls, fine young girls, Captain, only fifteen years old, very nice, plenty dance, plenty . . . . . . that's right gentlemen, get in Sir, Kiedive Gardens, alright Sir, I come from South Wales near London, Captain, very good family Sir."

His persistence pays off and we take his cab.

The Arab horses are woefully treated, with impatient drivers working their whips unmercifully to make them trot or gallop faster. Often the cab is overloaded with seamen or soldiers with little or no thought ever given to the tired old horse. They keep going incessantly around the streets with little or no rest between customers.

On our trip we see the local life: country carts built from wooden frames on enormously high and wobbling wheels, little donkeys ridiculously overloaded, and herds of skinny goats apparently eating the sandy road. We pull up at a small country inn on the banks of the Nile; the sand has given us a thirst and the beer is cool. We watch the dhows drift by on the sluggish brown stream, much as they have done for 2,000 years. Our cabman says it takes five days to get from here to Cairo on the river but, like the rest of them, he probably knows nothing at all about it. Very little has changed here in the past 2,000 years except the introduction of licensing hours and the beer which, I believe, was that much better than it is today and could be drunk from proper glasses and not the bottle.

We continue with our tour, passing one of the forts built by Alexander the Great which now looks to be in need of builders. Suddenly, we are transplanted from the sandy waste of the desert to the Khedive Gardens – Kew Gardens in summertime – which are a blaze of colour and sweet with roses; here and there are miniature ponds and waterfalls, and some genuine green grass.

The catacombs smell as musty as a disused forepeak, so we drive back to the Bourse[v] with its fine shops and crowds of Australian troops. Sitting for 20 minutes at an outside café table will give you every opportunity for inspecting the wares of as many hawkers; several of their goods are of a kind quite unobtainable in Woolworths. The hawkers are one of the main features of Alexandria; they even spread themselves out to the ships in the harbour from the moment the anchor goes down until she sails.

Jock McPherson is a full-blooded Arab who claims to have come from Greenock. He will sell you anything from a box of cigarettes, where only the top two layers can be smoked, to a bottle of whisky that proudly bears the label 'as drunk by the Royal Family'. I have my doubts as to whether the royal family will have ever drunk methylated spirit of the poorest quality. There is nothing Jock will not do or sell if there is enough profit in it, from scaling the ship's boilers to painting her complete hull. These people would have the skin from their mother's corpse if it were saleable, but I should say their business methods are a little more above board than many of our London 'financiers' or shipowners. At least the Arab will not cheat his own employees quite so much.

We sail from Alexandria and return to Gibraltar to land the naval gun crew and the gun which, because of their scarcity, will be transferred to another eastbound ship. It is now the middle of January and we are heading west in ballast across the Atlantic, bound for the dreaded Canada once again. A winter's passage in this class of tramp, or should I say government store ship, is never going to be pleasant.

It takes us 19 days to reach Saint John in New Brunswick. There is no heating in the cabins and our bunks lie close to the bare steel of the ship's side. In the Bay of Fundy the actual temperature is not as low as in other parts of eastern Canada, although with it being very damp any temperature below zero feels that much colder. No one has been fitted out with any warm clothing for these Artic conditions.

The weather grows colder and colder as the vessel punches up the bay in the north-westerly gale and the blinding snowstorms. The seas are steep and high with the spray freezing instantly as it falls onto the deck and the open bridge. Life must be very hard on the timber schooners and small barques that are also beating their way up into the bay. With the temperature ten degrees below zero, the ship becomes a white mass of ice and snow. Before we can anchor, a stream of boiling water must be played onto the hawse pipe and windlass. Chunks of ice have to be broken out and passed through the manhole door of the frozen freshwater tanks in order to get some water. Just think, three weeks ago it was almost hot in the Mediterranean…

The captain faces being hauled over the coals for a 'questionable expense' – buying some cheap paraffin oil stoves, which smell exactly like cheap oil stoves often do. These expenses must be reduced if the shipowner is to pay his shareholders their 150% dividend, but at least we are that little bit warmer.

You can guess that my opinion of Saint John is simply not printable when I tell you that whilst ashore one evening I slip over on the confounded slippery streets and break a good bottle of whisky. I am glad to be departing from this port after we have loaded a cargo of ammunition, oats, and hay. The ship – her decks piled high with a solid frozen mass of rubbish and coal dust – looks wretched under the clear moonlit skies that accompany these intensely cold nights. It is really beyond a joke to come off watch from the bridge and to see one's frozen oilskin standing upright on its own after taking it off.

Three days later it becomes comparatively mild and the ice starts to melt. We have one bit of trouble on the homeward passage when a Spanish fireman hit a Russian over the head with a fire axe; caught up in the resulting melee were a

Mexican, a Swede, a Greek, and a Malay. This cosmopolitan collection is typical of the British mercantile marine in the time of war. These so-called seamen are paid £8 per month, which is exactly the same as a certified and experienced British third officer, but the officers don't have a trade union!

The daily press is quite concerned about the ruinously high rate of wages being paid. One newspaper actually stated that a ship's crew had recently signed on with the enormous wages of £8 and ten shillings per month, the highest wages ever given to seamen in the history of the British mercantile marine. It thus raises the question as to how the company can possibly continue to reward its shareholders with their 100% dividend. No mention is ever made of the vastly increased cost of living, or the wretched position of the poor ship's third officer, who has little choice but to continue working for the same wages as the seamen. Politicians talk of merchant seamen as being the 'jugular vein' of the nation, providing of course they keep on working properly and do not make too many wage demands.

By the beginning of 1916, ship owning had become a highly profitable business with generous dividends being paid to the shareholders. Mr Bonar Law,[vi] who was the Chancellor of the Exchequer at the time, had invested heavily in shipping and found his shipping dividends to be most gratifying. At least he had the courage to say so in his speech to the House on the subject. 'I don't like talking about my shipping investments,' he said. 'I am ashamed of them. My investments have been in ten different companies under different management. It is true they were all in tramp steamers, but I am not quite sure if they make more profit than the liners. The sum invested in these ships was £8,110. In 1915, the dividend was £3,624, and in 1916 I received £3,874.'

He continued his speech by telling the House that when one of the tramp steamers in which he had invested £200 had been sunk or sold, although he couldn't remember which, he had received a payment of £1,000, despite having been previously paid a very handsome dividend. He also mentioned 'a division of surplus capital' from a shipping company that earned him £1,050 from an initial £350 investment.

Freight rates were tremendously high in 1916. In one instance, the value of cargo being shipped from England to the States was $1,050 yet the freight charge was $2,500. The shipowners netted between 100% to 400% return on their capital at the expense of the sea staff, who took most of the risks for wages that were insignificant when compared with the huge profits being made. When taking the cost of living into account, the wages from the captain down to the lowest paid seaman were not one penny more than in pre-war times. The men of the mercantile marine will receive no pension for war disablements because we are civilians and not soldiers, but a certified officer is of far more importance to the country than a soldier. The alternative would be to recognise the mercantile marine as a fighting force and then we would have the benefits of gratuities and pensions.

During this profitable yet dangerous period of the war, an appeal was sent out by the Merchant Service Guild[vii] to every shipowner in the country to raise a fund for their employees interned in Germany. The result of this appeal revealed the true generosity of these prosperous war profiteers towards their seagoing employees; the sum of £471 and eight shillings was collected, a miserly three pence per each dependent. The shipowner chose not to play the game then, has not done so before, and has not done so since, and that is the end of it. I apologise for having broken out with this tirade against the shipowner, for it may not interest you in the slightest and it does little good. A certain type of shipowner will only laugh at what I have said, suggest that I am a crazy fool, and go on overloading his ships and underpaying his employees just the same.

There being 40 steamers at anchor in Le Havre roads upon our arrival, we receive orders to proceed to Dungeness West roads through the Folkestone Gate, a narrow wartime channel through which all ships must pass to enter or leave the Dover Straits. It is surprising how many vessels can accumulate when the traffic is held up for a few hours. I have seen 150 merchant ships collected together in Yarmouth roads due to delays. We don't stay long before crossing the Channel again to Boulogne and anchoring in the outer harbour where, with a valuable cargo, we will be safe once more. Unfortunately, this harbour is also full, so despite it being a dirty winter night with heavy snow, we are soon ordered back out to sea again.

When I come off watch at midnight, our baker is moaning that his bread won't rise. I haven't been in my bunk for more than ten minutes when a sharp metallic noise similar to that of a telephone can be heard followed by a huge explosion as we are hit by torpedoes from both sides. The shock throws me from my bunk onto the deck. My porthole is blown in, but the cabin lamp still burns with the glass intact. The pasty face of the baker shows up through the opening where my heavy teak cabin door should have been.

'Well,' I say, 'did you get your bread to rise?'

'Bread,' he says, 'yes, it's risen alright, through the galley skylight. What's wrong?'

'What's wrong? By the sound of the water coming in I should say she's sinking fast. You had better hop it for your boat.'

I must say I am a bit confused; there can be no other reason for putting on my bowler hat and leaving my camera on the settee. I have planned for such an emergency by packing all my papers, a few treasured relics, a clean collar and tie, some tobacco, and shoe polish into a small attaché case. With this slung over one shoulder and my sea boots clutched in one hand, I run along the smoke-filled alleyway. A sixth sense warns me of imminent danger and I stop to strike a match. A yawning chasm is right at my feet; I catch a glimpse of a body floating on the coal-scummed water far below. The low side bunker hatches and coamings have been blown up and the deck split wide open. Nothing can be done, so I cautiously reach around the corner for the short iron ladder leading to the boat deck.

The stokehold watch below have all been killed instantly except for one poor chap who has dragged himself up the fiddley[viii] ladder with his thigh bone protruding through his trousers. Some of the crew in running from forward to the boat deck have fallen headlong into the bunkers to be drowned like rats in a trap. The wooden Marconi house on the bridge has collapsed inwards leaving the radio operators to climb through the deckhead. There is no time left but to make for the boats. Only a Swede and the two wireless men are standing by my boat, which we quickly lower with the two operators sitting inside. The senior radio operator has the seat of his striped pyjamas missing; the junior operator is so nervous that he cut the boat's painter as soon as it hit the water, allowing them to drift off, gesticulating wildly, into the snow and the darkness beyond.

'Where's the captain? Where's the captain?' I hear the old mate yell.

'In the bloody boat, and waiting to shove off!' someone answers.

There is no time to dawdle, for the ship's decks are awash. I jump off into the pitch black and land on somebody's foot to the sound of some horrible language. We shove off hurriedly, knowing that from this very moment our pay will stop until we get another job. It does seem a bit mean, but those dividends must be paid. The hard case second engineer, who had tried to be paid off in Le Havre, appears to be the only person happy to be getting off the ship. I get quite friendly with him because he is the only one in the crowd with any money.

Eventually we get picked up by a tugboat and taken into Boulogne, where the captain lines us up on the quayside for a roll call. We're as cheerful as cold boiled rice on a winter's morning, and it's certainly one of those. Shivering on the quayside whilst the authorities fill out forms, the man with the protruding thigh bone now has a chance to die.

The third engineer, normally a cheerful soul but hurt about the feet after getting out of the engine room, has managed to procure a bottle of whisky from a steward aboard the hospital ship. I climb into an adjacent bunk and we make the best of what is left of an eventful night. The people on the hospital ship have little concern for 'expenses' and serve us brandy and Bovril to combat the cold and to soothe our nerves.

In the afternoon we make the cross-Channel crossing onboard a heavily escorted steamer that was blown in half and sunk on her return journey. There is some delay at Folkestone in examining us; we look like members of a raided nightclub after a fancy dress ball, with some of us in uniform and some in rags. The six-foot senior wireless operator is wearing a short flannel hospital coat with sky blue trousers, the junior operator is in uniform with my sea boots, and the third engineer has remained in his greasy boiler suit with a tasselled yachtsman's cap. I look the most respectable with my bowler hat, as if I were some clerk going to work after a hectic night out. We are certainly a weird looking collection for a shipwrecked crew.

Outside the docks a gentleman offers to pay our tram fares to the station; God bless him and his family for a dozen generations, and the Canadian soldier who gave me a packet of cigarettes. Generally though, the people of Folkestone just stare and grin at us. I suppose they think we are some advertising stunt. On our arrival in London, the crew is sent to the Sailors' Home for the night, but the place is so full with shipwrecked seamen that our lot have to sleep on the floor. I go home by the tube to North London. The ladies on the train eye me rather disdainfully, as if it were high time I was in khaki. I can't say I can blame them entirely, for I don't look like a shipwrecked mariner in the slightest.

The next day I drift into the shipping company's office only to be asked by the manager with a fatuous smile whether I have come for my money; not one single word of congratulations at having got clear of their mouldy old packet. Perhaps I'm speaking out of turn, yet I cannot help but thank Germany for putting her under. Money with a capital 'M' is all these people can think about, and very sensible of them it is too!

I believe this company lost their entire fleet during the war, doubtless at a good profit for their shareholders. We are told by the press that the men of the mercantile marine are doing wonderful work and showing great heroism. I am so glad to be a hero, but my hat still fits! The mercantile marine is doing what it has always done, albeit with a few extra difficulties and a lot of unpaid extra work thrown in. It is our duty to swell the dividends first and feed the country second – this is called 'patriotism'. Our only real compensation is that the ordinary pre-war monotony of sea life is relieved just a little.

5   THE THIRD MATE

When we got ashore after that torpedoing business, the old chief officer told me that he was finished with the sea and that he would sooner sweep the streets than go through all that again. You can imagine my surprise therefore when I joined another of the company's vessels as second mate a fortnight later to find the old chief officer on board. It's a great pity the poor chap didn't stick to his decision, for he lost his life on the following voyage. British seamen being in short supply, we take on a deck crew of Malays and some Arab firemen.

To save money, our manager tries taking advantage of the shortage of certified mercantile marine officers by sailing without a third officer. He's hoping the chief officer and I will do double the work for the same meagre wages, all in the name of patriotism, but I tell him I would see him in Hell first. It would be impossible for us to maintain the vigilant lookout that is absolutely necessary in wartime on board a 5,000-ton ship with a Malay deck crew, and with the mate and me working 12-hour watches every day. The manager would have sacked me on the spot if he had dared, but as it was he found a third officer, a young fellow 73 years of age, who was as strange a character as you would ever wish to meet.

Arriving from New York, where he had had some job in the Customs, he tried to 'join up', but was too drunk at the recruiting office to be favourably received, although he had four sons in France and was as hardy as any young soldier aged 20. He decided to stay at a hotel in Cardiff courting Mother Booze and the barmaid until his locker was empty. 'I may be getting on in years,' he said to me on joining the ship, 'but there's not so many who can stand on their heads when they're over 70!' He promptly stood on his head to prove the point and took five shillings off me before returning to the pub.

On this voyage to Halifax, Nova Scotia, we keep close to the Welsh and Irish shores and right under the shadow of the beautiful cliffs and caves around Mizen

Head, where the sweet scent of the wet turf is wafted seaward. The third officer keeps himself busy in his spare time on the 12-day passage with his hobby of 'laundry work'. His cabin is festooned with yellowish rags that were once his clothes, but are now too far gone and tatty for the poor old chap to expose to the public view. At sea he wears homemade white canvas trousers and socks upon which he has sewn patches.

We arrive at Halifax in the early morning and commence loading some of the few thousand tons of flour we are to take to France. As often happened, by the time evening came the old third mate, whose cabin is opposite mine, has had many imaginary visitors to see him.

'Good evening, Captain!'

'Oh good evening, do come in and have a drink,' he would reply to himself. A glass would chink, and then he would ramble on to his imaginary old shipmates about strange happenings and past voyages when he had been master of Nova Scotia schooners and brigs in the Spanish and South American dried fish trade. He would speak of shipwrecks and mutinies in which his wife, who had borne him 11 children, had taken an active part. He remembered the schooners *Rose Marie* and the *San Juan*; the brig *Modiste*, abandoned at sea; and the *Mystery*, which was lost by fire. His body is scarred by make-believe wounds from bullet and knife. Poor old chap – I liked to listen to his stories because sometimes I imagined I might just be hearing the truth. He went ashore later that night; the police brought him back to the ship just before we sailed. He seemed quite unconcerned, smoking his vile old pipe and totally out of his mind.

The cargo being loaded and the hatches battened down, a gang of naval ratings work for a couple of days making chocks and then securing the four 80-foot motor launches we load on deck. These are the M. L. Boats,[i] 'Joy Yachts' or 'Petrol Punishers' as they are nicknamed. About 550 of these boats were built, mostly in Canada and Bayonne in New Brunswick, but they were not particularly successful because their petrol consumption was around 50 gallons per hour for a speed of 19 knots. Not only that, they were very costly to build, had insufficient beam for their length, and lacked any strength in a seaway. I know a little about their construction because I later lived on and looked after one of these launches that had been converted into a yacht.

We leave Halifax shortly before a terrific explosion[ii] in the harbour. Our destroyer escort is picked up 200 miles west of the Scilly Isles but lost an hour later in thick fog, only to next be seen inside Portsmouth harbour. The French ports being too congested to receive more ships, we lie at anchor for ten days in the Solent before finally crossing the Channel and discharging our cargo of flour in Calais. We are then sent back to Cardiff for bunkers.

The shipping company manager hasn't forgotten me. I am informed that an 'older servant' of the company is here to relieve me and that he has agreed to sail without a third officer. Good luck to him; unfortunately the ship was sunk on her next voyage, so I wasn't too sorry to be out of it. The last I saw of the old third mate was in the pub shortly after he had discharged himself from the ship. 'They may get an older man than me,' he told me, 'but by God they won't find one tougher!'

6 THE CROSS-CHANNEL RUN

The 18 months from the middle of 1916 to the beginning of 1918 are the most pleasant and happy times I have in my 20 years at sea. Our steamer is a poor class tramp of about 4,000 tons, but she has been built for a special trade and with a good speed, which are the very reasons for her being requisitioned as a Military Transport to ferry troops and war material across to France.

She has the worst accommodation of any ship for her size I have ever sailed in, but one can put up with that easily enough if the other conditions are fairly good. She is commanded by an easygoing Irishman who leaves things pretty well to his officers once he has found them to be trustworthy and conscientious. A really competent tramp steamer shipmaster is a man in a hundred. He must have a strong nerve, a brain of no mean order, and be a thoroughly good businessman.

We are kept busy all the time apart from the periods of unavoidable delays. We make 112 trips across the Channel in 18 months, firstly from Avonmouth to Rouen and then from either Portsmouth or Southampton to most of the Channel ports in France. The cargoes are a miscellaneous jumble of war material, from motor lorries, cycles, steam wagons, disinfectors, and railway wagons, to guns, provisions, and troops. We make the return passages either light ship or with scrap from the battlefront such as damaged guns or wrecked lorries and wagons. At a later stage the ship carries over 300 army tanks, 30 per trip, from Portsmouth dockyard to Le Havre. Occasionally we load big and beautifully fitted out hospital Pullman cars, four of them to a complete train that were stowed one on each side of the fore and main decks. Nearly all this war material, except the tanks and trains, is loaded and discharged using the ship's own gear, no mean feat with some of the lorries weighing over ten tons and with our heavy lift derrick being more or less a homemade affair. I think we held the record for doing no damage whatsoever to a single machine during the whole period.

Most of the other vessels running in conjunction with us are sunk either by mine or torpedo, and some with a tragic loss of life. It isn't until April 1917 that we have any naval escorts. We never see a submarine, but do pass one or two floating mines a little too close for comfort. It will make little difference if we run into trouble; our decks are so cluttered with lorries and so forth that getting to the lifeboats quickly, either from the crew quarters forward or the troops quarters aft, is virtually impossible.

However happy these times are though, the wages still do not do justice to our work:

> A moment please! The third officer's wages on this Military Transport are five shillings more per week than the Arab firemen who, except for the donkeyman (Serang) cannot even speak English! The chief officer, a position just now of very considerable responsibility and this being a troop carrier with cargoes of great value – well, he receives just five shillings a week more than his Chinese steward who waits on him! I simply ask you if that is fair? And now you will see what I meant when I said the mercantile marine should have made money while they could! The homogeneous collection called British subjects who manned the ships did well enough getting practically the same pay as the certificated ship's navigating officers, the engineer officers being the same. I ask you confidentially, ain't it sweet? Really I feel ashamed to tell you such things, because naturally you will wonder what kind of men we are to be only worth such a wage! Well, I simply don't know – we don't bother about it, that's all. We have no organisation or anything; we must simply must take what is given us.

The winter of 1917 is a severe one with many gales and great submarine activity. The chances of collision and stranding are decidedly odds on with the navigation lights on the ships unlit and with the lighthouses ashore extinguished. We have one or two horribly narrow squeaks from the former. In one month alone there are 16 collisions in the English Channel, and between February and May, 1,600,000 tons of shipping are sunk.

I feel really sorry for the soldiers when we are sailing as a troopship from the Bristol Channel in these gales. By the time we are off Trevose Head in Devon, most of them look to be more ready for a hospital than fighting in the trenches in France. Even the military sentries, who are supposed to be guarding our lifeboats, have abandoned their posts because of seasickness. They would all far rather be at the battlefront than on this steam packet off Land's End and heading for Rouen.

The lovely valley of the Seine has never before seen such river traffic. The Fishguard railway ferry, now a white hospital ship, heads downriver loaded with her sad freight, whilst a cross-Channel packet overtakes us, her decks a mass of khaki from bow to stern. A well-known Isle of Man steamer packed with troops lies astern of us; following the hospital ship, a Newhaven packet full of homeward bounders – who give derisive shouts as we pass – heads west towards the Channel.

We pass the castle at Tancarville perched high on the hillside and the canal locks, and head upriver. I've been up and down the Seine dozens of times, winding through miles of woodland and lush water meadows fronted by rows of tall poplar trees. To me, the Seine is always lovely. In the springtime the riverbanks are covered by drooping willows and wild flowers; a stately chateau surrounded by ancient velvety lawns and a blazing riot of flower gardens will occasionally peep into view. In the summer I have seen the apple orchards with tethered cattle grazing between the trees, the twisting country lanes with bare-legged and ragged girls driving pigs towards weatherworn farmhouses, and the fields of hay being harvested by the farmhands and children. Now it is winter and there is a terrible traffic on the river. We change the river pilot at Villequier, a neat little village with white houses and cafés nestling under some beautiful woods.

We arrive at Rouen and berth in the middle of town, just above the transporter bridge. There are no docks at Rouen, just several miles of wharves and jetties extending down the river from the city and filled with every type of vessel imaginable. Shortly after making fast, Mac (the third officer) and myself are sitting in a café across the cobbled street drinking our rum and coffee whilst watching the troops disembark and march away. Fortunately, there is no marching away for us because we are civilians responsible for maintaining these shipping dividends – so we have another rum!

As civilians, we also have our share of risks and troubles – some I wouldn't wish upon any soldier – such as dealing with 'paravanes', confounded contraptions for cutting moored mines adrift and throwing them clear of the ship. These things were introduced to the ship in 1917 and seemed very nice in theory, but not in practice. They gave me instant promotion in a way I didn't like at all when the chief officer's legs were cut off, as if with a giant pair of scissors, on the first voyage we had them on board. You couldn't have wished to meet a better officer.

The naval authorities will flatly contradict me. The demonstrating officer with his large crew of trained naval men will prove that the paravanes are quite simple to operate in smooth water and in daylight, but let that same officer try lowering the two-ton iron shoe down the stem, and put the 'otters' over the side on a dirty and black winter's night. The vessel is rolling, the decks are slippery, and the freezing sea spray is not only drenching the forecastle head, but also the four wet, frozen, shivering, and sulky West Indian crewmembers ordered to help me. If I were one of those dashing tars full of reckless courage and daring, then things might be different, but in reality I am a decidedly timid man; I ought to be singing in the village choir instead of having to rig one of these confounded things on a freezing winter's night. Eventually, we are successful in getting our paravane into the water. The speed of the ship will open out the otters about 20 feet away from the ship's side and hopefully cut the wires of any mine that should come in too close. I must say I've bought better inventions than this at Woolworths, but I don't intend to be rude to the inventor, a Commander[i] whose name I cannot remember. My own invention contains a double whisky, a double gin, a dash of vermouth, a shot of apricot brandy, a couple of raw eggs, and soda water. Which invention is the most easy to work and would do you the most good on a winter's night? The answer to the question is very simple!

I am able to get home fairly frequently on this run. The railway carriages from Portsmouth are always full of bluejackets. I gather from their conversations that the Germans must have had thousands of submarines; every sailor I meet on the train has either sunk one or helped to sink one! On one journey, I was sitting in the overcrowded compartment wedged between two ladies of generous proportions and opposite a little man wearing a bowler hat when down came my suitcase from the luggage rack straight onto his head. I must say he took it extremely well. When his face appeared again from under his crushed bowler, he told me that he lived in Margate and that I shouldn't worry too much because they were used to things falling on them in Margate. That's the spirit! It being a hot summer afternoon and with the ladies telling me I should be wearing khaki, I left the carriage with its 13 other passengers at the next stop and travelled the rest of the way first class.

I can never understand why civilian strangers are allowed to wander around Portsmouth dockyard in wartime when it is impossible to enter the docks at Avonmouth without showing some identity papers. Why there should be no security at such an important place as Portsmouth Naval Dockyard completely baffles me. The dockyard officials will say they have their own methods and know very well who is in the yard, but that is simply rubbish. It is the easiest thing in the world for a civilian in plain clothes to gain entry into the yard, walk all around and walk out again, particularly during the hours of darkness. The fact of the matter is red tape; everything must be done in a certain way, however ridiculous.

It has been said that information on vessel movements in the Bristol Channel is as leaky as the lifeboats of some cargo steamers. We were once given an immediate top-secret job and rushed round from Southampton to Avonmouth, with our sealed orders regarding our next port to be opened at sea. However, when the third officer travelled to Bristol the night before sailing, he was told by three different people that the ship was bound for Dublin. Someone told us exactly the same thing in the locks before entering the Bristol Channel. When the envelope was opened off the Welsh coast, Dublin was our destination!

On one voyage, after reaching Trevose Head off Devon, we were sent back to anchor in Barry roads for ten days, so intense was the activity of the enemy submarines at the mouth of the Bristol Channel. This was one of the most dangerous months of the war with the food supply in the country running very low. For the navy, it was a time of great worry and strain as they concentrated their full forces to save the country from starvation. On one particular trip, a destroyer, or what was left of it after hitting a mine, was made fast alongside. Fifty-two lives were lost – a ghastly mess – and yet the dividends for the merchant shipping companies still boom.

We make several trips from France to Newport with millions of empty shell cases. Despite it being winter with the weather really cold and windy, the women and girls employed to stack the shells onto the quay like to dance about on top of the 20-foot piles dressed only in low-necked blouses, skirts, and thin stockings. Perhaps the repartee from the few men working aboard is enough to keep them warm, but the sight gives us mere sailormen an attack of the shivers!

I must say we are not in an enviable position on board the ship during the air raids in the French ports with the docks being a target, but it is safer to stay aboard than to seek the shelter of a dugout ashore. During the war Dunkirk had 214 air raids with 7,514 projectiles dropped onto the town, which goes to show the French ports in 1917 were none too healthy places to visit. One winter's evening, when the ship was anchored off Calais, a destroyer hailed us with orders to shift our anchorage position to as close inshore as possible as they were expecting a raid by enemy destroyers. Very nice too, for we were between the devil and the deep blue sea so to speak. It turned out to be an air raid instead with their target a large oil tanker at anchor nearby. I watched this raid, and a fine sight it was, whilst sharing a drop of whisky with the captain. Turning in a little later, I slept well despite the noise, so there couldn't have been much wrong with me in those days. It isn't the danger or a bit of hardship that causes the loss of sleep; it is the fear of unemployment in peacetime and the lack of overtime that does the damage.

In the spring of 1918, the vessel is ordered round to Barry, where 2,000 tons of permanent sand ballast are discharged, her troop quarters scrapped, and the ship turned into a collier. The good times are over.

7   A Wartime Tramp's Voyage

As the chief officer, I sometimes have the tedious job of censoring the mail, which includes my own letters to my wife. It seems a senseless exercise to censor my very own ramblings, because I know all the rules, but the letters won't arrive home unless they bear the marks and deletions of the official ship's censor. Having said all that, some of the correspondence between our West Indian crew and the local Welsh ladies needs a great deal of censoring, believe you me!

The mate's job in a tramp steamer (or does it sound better if I call myself the chief officer?) is never pleasant when loading a cargo of coal in Barry dock. This time it is worse than usual with the continuous rain making the thick coating of coal dust that covers the decks from bow to stern very beastly. The quaysides are hidden under a filthy black slush and the docks look bleak and gloomy.

At frequent intervals, day or night, we must warp the vessel along the quay to allow the fixed coal loading chutes to work another hatch. We have only four West Indian sailors in a watch, so two must be at each end of the vessel when she is shifting with me assisting in handling the greasy wire rope moorings. A West Indian crew seems the only one available at the moment, but they are proving to be not at all suitable and will take advantage of the situation whenever they can. With regard to the West Indians and the Caribbean islanders, the Sailing Directions state:

> They do not undertake any kind of work but are content to loll about the beaches, or sleep in their little grass huts, from one week's end to another. Their extreme want of energy and their existence as far as alimony goes is a mystery to the European.

I cannot blame the crew for wanting to loll about the beaches, but they can't do it here; my job is to keep them awake and to try to get a little work done occasionally. With the frequent shifting of the ship under the coal chutes, there are no regular meals on board. As usual, the ship's chandler supplies the stores at the last moment, but because it is after 5 p.m., the crew doesn't want to take them on board. The chief officer has his hands full with one thing and another; the last of the cargo is being shipped and the loadline must be carefully watched to ensure the vessel is not overloaded, he must keep an eye on the seamen in case they get away ashore and jump ship, and he must watch the stores closely to see nothing is stolen.

The disciplinary rules and regulations for this class of merchant ship during the latter stages of the war became peculiar and unclear. It seemed that the crew could do more or less what they liked, including refusing to carry out a quite legitimate order. They could not, however, refuse to sail the ship. In the event of any trouble, the Naval authorities merely referred you to the police and the police referred you back to the Naval authorities!

Even in cases of rank insubordination and assault, as long as they did not refuse to sail, the law would have nothing to do with it. It was an entirely different kettle of fish if a hard case officer assaulted a member of the crew, just see what happened then! The truth of the matter, and I can understand the reasons behind it, is that the ship must sail at all costs and without delay. Hard lines on the master and officers of these poorer class boats with their West Indian crews – the ship *must* sail.

One way or another, the ship leaves the locks on time loaded with 6,000 tons of coal under her hatches and eight railway wagons and two seaplanes on deck. I have had only three hours rest in the last 48 hours, so when the orders are received to put the paravanes over the side on this blowy night, I feel inclined not to fool about with them. It is really unfortunate that a slight heave on a wire at the wrong moment rendered the apparatus temporarily useless. I have no choice but to go and lie down for an hour or two! The ship is only going round to Milford Haven, a seven-hour run, to join a convoy there. We are, of course, under sealed orders, but everyone seems to know we are bound for Port Said.

The convoy presents an imposing spectacle leaving Milford Haven: 27 steamers of all types with our ship in the middle of them. The collection is more like a flock of alarmed sheep than a fleet of vessels, with no one following their directions properly for getting into formation; we also had a job finding our place. One way or another everyone eventually gets into their correct position and we set off for the nine-day voyage to Gibraltar. We are ordered not to throw any rubbish over the side; a trail of floating rubbish might give a clue to enemy submarines as to what course the convoy is taking. After three weeks in Barry dock though, the decks on our vessel are one big evil-smelling rubbish heap, ever-increasing in size, which according to the 'orders' we must carry to east of Suez! Some misguided persons, however, throw it over the side at night!

A 'Rock Scorpion' selling different types of liquor from his bumboat greets us in Gibraltar. One brand of whisky has labels on its bottles telling us 'As drunk in the House of Commons', which goes a long way to explaining some of the queer speeches we hear from these chambers. The second engineer, who ought to have known better, purchases some brandy reputedly consumed by the 'Nobility'. The bumboat man is indeed fortunate he has moved a short distance away from the ship's side; a couple of the 'Nobility' bottles miss his head by only inches on their return journey back towards his boat.

From Gibraltar we join a convoy to Bizerte, a voyage of about 750 miles. We head south across the Straits and keep close to the Moroccan shore, passing Ceuta and Tetuan, one of the few places in this country where we are permitted to make a landing. We see lofty mountains a few miles inland, and then it's on to Cap Falcon and the Gulf of Oran, where the Algerian coast commences. This is a country of lakes and marshes, enormous salt deposits, and gigantic trees. Centipedes abound and I receive a good bottle of wine in exchange for an old pair of boots in Algiers, the capital. This coast is quite well lit as we pass Caps Matifou, Bengut, and Carbon, but no lights show at night on the ship. The weather is rather too warm for comfort as the small porthole in one's cabin must be closed and screened at night.

Beyond Algiers the coast seems about as wild and desolate as me. All the cargo gear has to be re-rigged and new derricks have to be shipped. With one man at the wheel and another continuously on the lookout, it leaves me with just the bosun and one seaman to do the job. Appearing in the distance as if it were an island, we sight Cap Bougaroun lying at the northern extremity of a mountainous promontory with the summits of Jebel Agilman and Jebel El Goufi in the background.

We finally reach Tunisia at Cap de Fer and enter the straits known locally as the Canal de la Galite between the mainland and the island of La Galite, with rugged cliffs, grassy slopes, and a few Sardinian fishermen living on the south side. After passing Cap Serrat, we round Cap Blanc and head south towards Bizerte Lake, which can only be entered by proceeding single file down a narrow channel. For six days the ship lies at anchor in this big inland lake that is surrounded by rolling downs and deep green olive groves. The break is pleasant enough, with us being allowed ashore to stretch our legs.

At the beginning of April we are underway again in another convoy, bound for Malta and Port Said. Our ship has been chosen as leader of the convoy and we have to give the signal to the other ships when it is time to zigzag. This has nothing to do with Zig-Zag cigarette papers, but is merely because we are father, and when father says turn we all must turn! A flag signal is first hoisted by a small apprentice boy to indicate the direction in which the convoy is to alter course, followed by a cork fender. When the fender is lowered, all the vessels must turn together. The process is repeated for the next alteration of course. On one unfortunate occasion, the boy became distracted and released the cork fender too early. It landed on the captain's head, nearly knocking him out, and all the ships turned as instructed except for us. A collision was very near indeed!

We pass to the north of Malta and arrive at the dreary city of Port Said where the ship is moored with both anchors down forward and her stern made fast to posts in the desert sand. Then follows ten days of discharging the coal; ten days of heat, flies, and the coal dust competing with sandstorms.

It is a relief to get away into the Suez Canal, although the canal provides little rest for the chief officer in this class of ship. I've been through the Suez Canal on many occasions and in various capacities, as a second officer of large vessels, as a first class passenger, as a quartermaster, but I find it particularly troublesome with this short-handed and grumbling West Indian crew. The vessel has to tie up to the bank at frequent intervals to allow spotless passenger ships to go past. One can almost hear the comments from the dozens of passengers and sahibs lining the rails as they look down upon us. We have come straight from the coal berth in Port Said and cannot start washing down the decks until we are clear of the canal. The filthiest of tramps standing next to a West End city gentleman could not have stood out more.

We pass the tents of the Armenian refugee camp gleaming eerily in the white moonlight and the great military camp at El Qantara is strangely silent. At a later period, I was second officer on a big ex-German steamer when we lay for a fortnight discharging hay at this very same camp in the Suez Canal.

By day the heat in the Red Sea is very intense; the sides of our small cabins and the deck above are bare steel, making the spaces like furnaces in which rest or sleep is almost impossible. There are no electric lights on this vessel, no fans, no ice, and when we come to rig the awnings for some shade, we find rats have eaten the canvas. One can put up with most things when on a good and regular trade in home waters, but living on this vessel in summer in the Red Sea becomes rather trying, especially when we have the usual poor quality tramp steamer food. It is, however, much better than being in Canada in winter, most decidedly so!

During the voyage between Suez Bay and Karachi, which is some 2,900 miles, the coal dust from the last cargo must be thoroughly swept up and the holds washed out so that they are clean and dry for loading wheat immediately upon our arrival. I find that I have more than enough to do in this heat as the chief officer with keeping my two four-hour bridge navigation watches and superintending the hatch work and cleaning out of the stinking hold bilges.

It becomes very busy when we arrive at Karachi. We load 6,664 tons of wheat in just two days and ten hours – 66,640 bags stowed by hand by five gangs of 60 labourers working continuously day and night. They use 16,000 woven mats and 30,000 wooden poles as dunnage to keep the hessian bags off the bare ironwork of the ship's structure. A gang of natives paints the ship's hull as it slowly sinks deeper into the water with the loading.

The usual crowd of curio sellers and fortune-tellers are on board. The prices have gone up, but you can still get a haircut, manicure, and your fortune read, all by the same man, for two shillings. He has a good deal to say about my head, but I suppose there's not a lot in it, otherwise I wouldn't be here!

We come away from Karachi on a Sunday afternoon and the following Sunday we are moored to a buoy off Aden discharging some of the wheat. Aden, like the Red Sea, is unbearably hot in this ship; upon my word, I have to think continuously of Canada to keep cool! On the passage up the Red Sea, the crew decides they like painting and by the time we enter Port Said, the ship is looking very spick and span. It doesn't last too long; a delay in assembling the northbound convoy sees us waiting alongside the coal tier where we are soon covered in a mass of coal dust once again.

Before we depart from Egypt, six bags of mail are delivered on board along with six down-at-heel gentlemen travelling DBS (Distressed British Seaman).[i] The convoy becomes an excellent target for prowling submarines with the inclusion of a very old steamer that is continually breaking down. We break away from the other ships and proceed round the south coast of Malta and then through St. Paul's Bay and the narrow and pretty Comino Channel into Valletta.

I like Malta; a large glass of pre-war whisky costs only sixpence and there are several other attractions. I decide to go ashore with Fatty, the third engineer, in one of those gondola affairs that ply the harbour. Fatty is anxious to see the Chapel of

Bones[ii], but being a bit late we take a cab. Our friendly driver is no different to other drivers; he takes us to some 'bones' alright, but these 'bones' are barely earning a living in a dance hall. Why is it that whenever a sailor charters a cab abroad, the driver will invariably lay the course to a whorehouse? We don't stop there because Valletta is a city with many more worthy sights than these to visit.

Herds of goats wander around the steep steps and narrow streets, and in the low doorways women and children can be seen making lacework by hand. The nursemaids pushing their prams in the Botanical gardens look quite nice, and there is a fine view over the harbour from the battlements. A quiet saloon bar will generally interest me more than a cathedral, but St. John's Co-Cathedral is an exception, the only uninteresting object being the mumbling old guide flitting about like a musty black bat. The floor of the church is made up of carved marble slabs, each one said to be the tomb of a crusader. Leading from the magnificent chancel are numerous chapels, each one dedicated to a nation. There are golden altar ornaments and the great brass gates that Napoleon once shipped away. The wonderfully painted dome is said to be the life's work of some old Master, but when we come to the realistic life-size painting of St. John the Baptist minus his head, we think time for refreshment is indicated.

The cargo of wheat is discharged at the rate of a thousand tons a day and stored where the Venetians once housed their galleys and prisoners.

We are accompanied by one other ship and two navy escorts to Sfax in Tunisia. The enemy submarines are reported to be particularly active and many ships have been sunk in the area. Sfax is quite a small place with French the only language and demijohns of cheap wine the only drink, but the bathing is delightful in the saltwater lake, warm at night and so salty that one cannot sink. One morning we had a false alarm: the chief engineer was mistaken for an enemy submarine when he was seen floating whilst taking his early morning dip! We load 6,000 tons of phosphate rock, beastly and dusty stuff, by means of an endless belt from the factory on the quay.

We head for Glasgow after leaving Sfax, keeping very close to the land before calling in at Bizerte on the way. It is very hot in the Mediterranean; the cabins are stuffy, and sleep is almost impossible. I haven't been below for long when up bobs a German submarine alongside with its gun trained towards us. The commander has the appearance of an evil fellow, but the lieutenant is a handsome man bearing an extraordinary likeness to myself. Both wear uniform caps, white sweaters, and have big prism binoculars slung around their necks. They spare sinking us because they think we look like the original Ark. 'Can't possibly sink such an antique, take it away captain and put it in a glass case!' The submarine vanishes with the knock on my cabin door to call me for my watch. These stuffy cabins can give you nasty dreams!

We arrive in Glasgow without any other incidents, in my dreams or otherwise:

> On arrival at Glasgow after this 12,000 mile voyage, it is found the vessel has been sold, though that is not the reason I left her. Perhaps it is that fatal restlessness that ruins any prospects one may have and which is all too common in the mercantile marine, or perhaps it is a very unnatural desire to see ones wife and little ones - sailors should not have such things because if they are going to have any home life at all, it simply means that they must be pillar to post men in the tramp steamer trade. The chief officer's busiest time is in port – how can he go home unless he throws up the job? He cannot do so – there's an end to it. A man longs to get out of the squalor of it all, just for a time. But putting jokes to one side, there is some kind of annual holiday on in this city of Glasgow, most extraordinary thing all the pubs are shut so why stay here? It's simply out of the question!

8   An Oil Tanker to Mexico

Her bow is made fast to a buoy off Hepburn-on-Tyne and from the waterman's boat it looks as if her stern must be somewhere down at Shields. The ship is currently one of the largest oil-carrying vessels in the world; she appears even larger than that to me. I am joining as second officer, the navigating man of this towering steel monster, the workings of which (as far as cargo is concerned) I have not the slightest idea.

The ship[i] is 527 feet long with a beam of 66 feet 6 inches; she draws 30 feet of water when loaded. She can carry about 16,000 tons of petrol in 24 separate compartments, or tanks as they are known, with each tank holding about 700 tons. In total that is about 3,750,000 gallons, which with the present price of petrol puts the value of the ship and her cargo at around £1 million. My wartime wage on this type of vessel is £6 per week,[ii] so I cannot say I am overpaid for doing most of the navigational work and having charge of the vessel's watch for eight hours every day. At the time of my writing this yarn, nearly ten years after the war, I would be lucky to be earning this amount, such is the Depression.

These large oil-carrying vessels, or tankers, are particularly strong; they need to be with their immense size and the nature of their cargo. The frames, or ribs, of the vessel run longitudinally instead of vertically as in ordinary shipbuilding. This gives a greater stiffness against bending at sea with the transverse strength being obtained by numerous cross-bulkheads that form the tanks; a continuous bulkhead runs from stem to stern, effectively dividing the vessel lengthwise into two halves.

I don't intend to be boring the reader with these details, but there are expansion trunks, summer tanks, endless pipelines, and valves of various colours, which look a good deal more complicated than they actually are in practice. The very volatile nature of petroleum and its great capacity for explosion when mixed with air renders a good ventilating system essential. Everything possible is done to reduce the risk of ignition; only electric lighting is used with the wiring double-sleeved, and the lights themselves are fitted with double glass jackets.

As is usual with these tankers, the powerful quadruple expansion engines, the oil-fired boilers and the engineers' accommodation are right aft. The navigation bridge and the officers' quarters are positioned well forward, leaving a clear 350 feet of deck between them. In this ship the expansion trunks and cargo tank tops are below the main deck, giving a sheltered passage in bad weather for the entire length of the vessel. I find it a great relief to get away from foreign crews and for a change to have a very good British crowd, nearly all of them coming from the Shetland Islands. We also carry a naval crew of six ratings to man two bomb-throwing guns amidships and a six-inch gun mounted on a platform at the stern.

Our destroyer escorts join us in Methil roads, Firth of Forth, and then we proceed north about through the Pentland Firth. It is blowing hard with a moderately heavy sea that hardly affects our lumbering great vessel, but tosses the destroyers about like corks to the extent they have to put back to the safety of port. Our course takes us up into the neighbourhood of Iceland before we turn south for a long and rough 5,500-mile passage of 21 days to Tampico.

The captain of this ship is a queer merchant, neither discipline nor teetotalism standing out conspicuously. He has no sextant and doesn't seem to bother his head with the ship's position even when passing through the Florida straits, where navigation for a ship of this size is not so easy. He has his good points; he plays the mouth organ well and will amuse himself for hours with his dancing doll toys.

The chief officer generally superintends the loading and discharging after first arranging the order for filling the tanks and the amount of cargo to be pumped into each tank. The second and third officers, assisted by the pumpman, will work on alternative four-hour cargo watches, day and night, to operate the valves that direct the flow of oil into the various tanks. On arrival in the port, two six-inch hoses are connected by screwed flanges to the ship's main pipeline. The signal is given to start the shore pump and a stream of fuel oil pours into the ship at the rate of 350 tons per hour.

The officer in charge watches until a tank is nearly full before gradually closing the tank valve to divert the cargo into the next tank to be filled. It is responsible work, but not difficult once one gets the run of the valves. Peering into the tanks will sometimes give temporary blindness, particularly with crude oil that has come straight from the earth before being refined into benzine, naphtha, petrol, and paraffin. Tar, asphalt, and Vaseline are the residues from the refining process. The fumes from the crude oil are unpleasant, tainting our food and water and turning all the white paint silver and metalwork on board to a sickly yellow colour.

The draught limit over the Tampico bar being 27 feet, we go down the coast and moor to buoys off the Tuxpan bar for more cargo. These bars, by the way, have nothing to do with licensed houses; some landsmen have peculiar notions of seafaring terms! At Tuxpan we pick up the shore pipeline from the ocean bed and complete loading. The big nine-inch manila hawsers with which we moor to the buoys are hauled in and we head up for New York to join the Atlantic convoy.

Our course takes us close along the low Florida shores, hugging the American seaboard from Palm Beach to the Frying Pan Shoals, close around Cape Hatteras, before slowing down off the glittering Jersey seaside resorts of Atlantic City and Ashbury Park so as to make our anchorage off Coney Island by daylight. The harbour in New York is very busy; every day some of the world's largest vessels pass our anchorage, packed with American troops in a hurry to get to Europe before the war is over.

Fortunately, we are unable to get ashore during our nine-day stay at anchor. I hate New York City after spending several days there waiting to join a ship. I had but little money and lodged at the top of some cheap hotel with nothing in the bedroom but a bed, a Bible, and directions on how to use the rope ladder stowed under the bed to reach the fire escape. The noise from the overhead trollies, or whatever they're called, and the general pandemonium of the city were enough to give anyone the creeps. And then there was a blizzard in which nothing could move at all for three days – too much like Canada for me!

Although our convoy leaving New York is an imposing one, it contains several underpowered craft which can just about steam and that's all, resulting in a 19-day passage across the Atlantic. Off the Scilly Isles, where the air is reported to be balmy, the convoy breaks up. We race up the English Channel along with two other great oil tankers. Between us, we are carrying 45,000 tons of fuel oil, just now a very precious cargo of vital importance to the country. We follow the line of buoys marking the swept channel along the east coast, keeping very much closer inshore than large ships would normally venture in ordinary times.

For a couple of days at Rosyth, we dole out driblets of fuel to salt-encrusted destroyers that dash in from the North Sea, come alongside, and dash off again fully fuelled 20 minutes later. The remaining 14,000 tons of oil are pumped out by the ship in 33 hours whilst lying alongside a jetty.

As soon as she is discharged we sail again for Tuxpan in Mexico, the land of white huts, palm trees, surf-beaten beaches, and oil storage tanks of 150,000 tons capacity. Somewhere in the mid-Atlantic, orders are received by wireless that we can switch on our navigation lights. The war is over, not that it will make much difference to us, except that with us all being old-timers on this ship, we can appreciate that very soon the service will be very overcrowded and that, at the very first possible moment, the wages will drop to bare subsistence level. We have not the faintest idea at that time what disaster is actually in store for us. I think there is no question at all that most personnel in the merchant service were financially very much better off during the war than after it.

From the buoy moorings a couple of miles out at sea off Tuxpan, we load a cargo of crude oil for a refinery at Puerto Mexico.[iii] The coast between these two ports is wild and rugged in places and is backed by the volcanic peak of Orizaba, the highest in Mexico at 18,400 feet, with a crater more than three miles across.

The town of Puerto Mexico at the mouth of the Coatzacoalcos River is an ill-kept sandy place on the slope of a range of hills. The buildings – except for the post office, the bank, and a faded yellow clapboard hotel – seem to be mainly constructed of galvanised sheet iron and wooden packing cases.

The inhabitants loll around under their enormous sombreros waiting for siesta time in this land that is poor for the dentist and good for the traveller selling insect powder. The atmosphere is very dull and uninteresting until a dapper army officer seated at the next table to ours on the wooden veranda of the dingy hotel stops sipping his wine, raises his pistol, and shoots dead a local gentleman walking on the pavement, or what is intended to be the pavement. No one takes the slightest bit of notice. The officer nonchalantly leans back in his rickety chair, holsters his pistol, and with a steady hand sips his wine again while we order another round of sweet warm American beer. Assassination seems to be quite a pastime around here; it's a pity it hasn't spread to England for the taxman or some other bore when they come knocking at one's door!

I said the place looks dull but it isn't. I don't suppose a more romantic country exists, with its unexpurgated modern history far more dramatic, thrilling, and interesting than Edgar Wallace at his best. What with bandits, revolutions, massacres, oil wars, huge fortunes, typhus fever, black-eyed sinuous women, and cowboys and the like, there's plenty going on, not that it would suit everyone. As a respectable tax-paying married man, it wouldn't suit me, but a few years ago…

The bandit is not quite the same thing as a company promoter or shipowner. The methods for obtaining the boodle are different, but the end result is just the same. The bandit has the advantage that if he dislikes nosy people enquiring into his business, he can have them tied between two wild horses which then gallop off in opposite directions. This was considered a light form of amusement for Pancho Villa,[iv] the most famous Mexican bandit of them all:

> The history of Mexico says:- "It is weirdly doubtful if any strange commingling of human and bestial passions ever merged on the form of man than in this fiend incarnate. But the milk and water viciousness and thirst for assassinations and wholesale executions of Carranza, the president; the barbaric cruelties of Zapata, another bandit, quite fade into insignificance compared with the acts of Villa whose record is unexampled and unparalleled in ancient or modern history."

One of the junior engineers on board has previously worked at a pumping station further north and he tells me these little shooting incidents and other atrocities cause no excitement whatever. An example of Mexican 'humour' was in dealing with a thief who had stolen a pair of boots. In the open plaza at Tuxpan, they lashed his amputated and booted feet to the stumps of his wrists, lashed his amputated hands to the stumps of his ankles, and then left him for a few hours to think the matter over. On the engineer's first duty night at this pumping station, the local foreman had an argument with his wife, which ended when he cut off her head on the engineer's doorstep. He had also seen 200 local village people killed by the followers of Villa, who rushed around completely naked in the general slaughter so they could distinguish themselves in the dark. The dead were left for days, and then thrown in a heap before being burned.

In 1911, Mexico's credit was stronger than any other Latin American country except Argentina. In 1914, Mexico produced half the world's supply of silver; had enormous amounts of gold, precious stones, and copper; grew fine cotton; and was rich in petroleum, but bandits and assassinations still ruled the day.

The guidebook says the railways are safe, but a passenger on board for the voyage down to Rio, a Birmingham man, who had been driving the big oil-fuelled engines on the Veracruz to Orizaba train, had a different tale. His train was often held up, with many passengers removed and hanged from the nearest trees. He had some particularly ghastly photos, some of them close-up, of rows of victims in various stages of strangulation.

With the country being in such a chaotic state, it was of vital importance that the oilfields should be kept going to supply petroleum for the fleet and the millions of motor lorries engaged in the war in France. The bandits could destroy the pipelines just for the fun of it unless it was made worth their while to leave them alone. It was made their worthwhile. Although the pumping stations had their furniture looted time and again, the machinery and the pipelines were left intact; the bandits had been paid! On board our ship, we are ordered to make sure that anyone of any note, such as Mexican customs officers and the like, are given free food and drink and made comfortable; they make the most of it and have the time of their lives.

This oil cargo is going to South America instead of the British fleet now that the war is over. Leaving Mexico, the ship's course is just north of the West Triangle Reef and across the Campeche Banks, where the water suddenly deepens from 180 feet to 9,000 feet. We pass the low sandalwood-covered Cayman Islands and along the north shore of Jamaica, with the famous Blue Mountains in the background. One of the first voyages I made as an officer in a steamer was round the West Indian islands, and very nice they are too if one has the time to look around. Unfortunately on that ship there was no time for anything but work and sleep.

The ship's course now lies between the islands of St. Lucia and St. Vincent and close along the coast of Barbados; from here we sight nothing of the vast sweep of the Brazilian coastline for nearly 4,000 miles until we make a landfall at Cabo Frio – the 'cold' cape – in latitude 23 degrees south. In this region the temperature can suddenly fall and furious wind and rain squalls are frequent; the ship's compass can be badly affected off this cape as there is often a considerable magnetic disturbance. As far as my recent experience goes, this part of the world is fine weather-wise, particularly so during our English springtime. The sea is generally smooth, rippled by the cooling south-easterly trade winds, streaked with miles of curious yellow fish spawn, and dotted with schools of playful porpoise. Close to the shoreline, the native fishermen can be seen in their little open craft that can be easily mistaken for floating bundles of rubbish. Sometimes the faded purple of the distant coastline appears to have miles of white buildings upon its shore; this effect is caused by the outline of dark trees against the dazzling white sand dunes, as in reality the coast is practically uninhabited.

I visited Bahia – one of the most antique, religious, and vicious cities in Brazil – in a steamer before the war. The city, which used to be the capital of Brazil before Rio de Janeiro, is finely situated around the entrance of the Recôncavo[v] of Bahia, a bay that is seven miles broad at its mouth and opens into a landlocked sea more than 100 miles in circumference. The inland sea is studded with islands of waving palms and dotted with gaudily painted native craft queerly rigged with huge mainsails and tiny jibs. The coastline is like a tropical garden with great purple mountains looming in the distance. Bahia, where everyone smokes long black cigars, including the little pot-bellied naked children, is the big tobacco port of Brazil.

The city is divided into two parts; the lower portion, Cidade Baixa, is just behind the waterfront at the foot of an almost perpendicular vegetation-covered cliff. Located here are the warehouses storing the tobacco, sugar, and coffee for export. Behind these is the noisy market, where enormously-proportioned ladies attired in the glariest and scantiest of costumes preside over their stalls, selling oranges, bananas, coconuts, beady-eyed little marmoset monkeys, gaily coloured birds, and rows of solemn-looking parrots.

Small mules driven by big half-naked Africans are hauling wagons of coffee and beeswax to the quay. Little donkeys, loaded with huge panniers on their backs and with a driver chewing sugar cane sitting cross saddle on their shoulders, vie for space on the busy roads. The wharves are crowded with all kinds of shipping moving gently with the incoming ocean swell.

Behind the *praia*,[vi] on top of the perpendicular cliff (made accessible by a wire rope tramway and passenger lifts), is the upper portion of the town. Here are narrow cobbled streets, good shops, and a noisy and reckless tramway system. It is a religious city with many Baroque-style churches, a cathedral with some fine broad plazas, and over 1,000 Candomblé[vii] temples for the African religion. Every other day seems to be a 'Saints' day, when the church bells are rung and fireworks let off; the place is not run along Sunday School lines.

On the hillsides overlooking the town are beautiful suburbs with large villas nestling in their tropical gardens. Differing from the usual one-storied flat-roofed houses found elsewhere in the tropics, these houses are built of stone and are up to five-storeys high. They have balconies in the Spanish style plastered in colour, many with the washing hanging out to dry.

> The most striking feature of this city, but not all, is the number of beautiful women. They may be of the rich class, dressed from the Rue de la Paix, or they may be in gawdy coloured rags, yet [...] they all have slim, beautiful figures, dainty features, great black eyes – which they know how to use, and lovely teeth. [...] In spite of all this bevy of beauty, as a matter of fact the prettiest girl[viii] I've seen wears specs, her little hands are very work stained, at present she is waiting for her false teeth; but there you are, tastes differ.[viii]

Our next port of call, except for two smaller ports, is Sao Pedro,[xii] which lies at the entrance to Lagoa dos Patos, a great inland lake with Porto Alegre at its end. No lovely harbour entrances to this place, just a crane sticking up above the horizon to show the whereabouts of the port. The land is completely flat with the town itself below sea level.

At Cabo Polonio in Uruguay, we round the corner into the mighty River Plate, nearly 120 miles wide at Lobos Island. In spite of its width, it is more or less a shallow river, a desolate waste of muddy water obstructed by innumerable shoals and sandbanks. The climate in this part of the world is not much better than it is in England, hot one day and cold the next. Some oil is discharged into lighters at Montevideo, as are the guns and ammunition, which are no longer needed and are not allowed up the river anyway.

We enter cattle country and Buenos Aires, the capital and main port of Argentina, from where frozen meat and a great quantity of cowhides are exported. The town is of one-storied houses, many trams and mosquitoes and with a strange smell about it. Women and roulette seem to be the main pastimes. The roulette rooms are well fitted out and quite orderly; the Pisandra, or street of women, just about touches the rock bottom of squalid depravity, dark and evil, and full of bemused layabouts from the city. The place is by no means safe.

When I was here on the steamers, I recall the local native Indian stevedores being rigged out in the strangest assortment of clothes, one of them in the first 'Plus Fours' I had ever seen, and little else besides a straw boater. Another man wore an old, but decidedly well-cut and tailored overcoat, ancient dancing pumps and a big sombrero.

On this occasion, it is inadvisable for us to go out of the dock gates into Buenos Aires. There is a general strike,[xiii] and all the ship's crew are considered to be blacklegs for discharging a part cargo of 800 barrels of asphalt. Our crew has been paid £40 in overtime and two large barrels of beer; the same quantity of cargo in Rio de Janeiro cost the company £500 to discharge with stevedores, lighters, and a floating crane. A lack of coal caused by the strike has meant that the great electric power station opposite the ship's berth is presently burning hundreds of tons of maize; there'll be a shortage of feed for the parrots homeward-bound!

Sailing craft are more in evidence here than they have been for years, the war having revived their fortunes. Two Liverpool schooners, the *Blytheswood* and the *County of Inverness*[xiv] – which were bought for £2,000 as coal hulks in 1916 – have both been re-rigged and are earning good profits. The barque *Marshona*[xv] that had been laid up for many years at Montevideo, was bought for £3,000, refitted for £7,000, and made a fast passage from the River Plate to New York and back, her owner refusing an offer of £30,000 for her. Her freight for linseed in one direction only was reported to be 28 ounces of gold per ton and she earned £19,000 freight on a cargo from South Georgia to Boston.

Down at the Boca district on the outskirts of the city are moored Norwegian barques, slovenly Italians, and smart Yankee schooners; the sailor town bars, the Irish Consul and the Dronning Maud, have a new lease of life. Under the grain elevator lies the old Sunderland ship, the *Cossack*, that was sold in 1908 for £7,250 and then changed hands in 1916 for £83,000. It's an ill war that blows no good to somebody!

After discharging our 'blackleg' asphalt, we steam upriver to supply Ammours frozen meat factory with several thousand tons of fuel oil. I find it really interesting to see the handling and freezing processes inside this wonderfully clean and well-organised factory.

Now we have a somewhat tedious 23-day passage back to the Mexican ports to load a full cargo of oil for the 5,000-mile passage to Hull. From August 1918 until May 1919, this ship has steamed over 50,000 miles with practically no time allowed for overhauling the engines.

The vessel is only going to be a few days in Hull, which will be busy ones for the officers, before she departs again for an 18-month voyage to the American coast. Since I've been away, I have had a son and I do not want him to be starting school before I see him. You can already guess what this means; despite the war being over and being extremely foolish from a financial point of view to leave a job that is better paid than most in the mercantile marine, I have to go. I have no choice, as I'm sure you will understand!

9 A Trip out East

The gentleman with the centre parted hair fingered his monocle and drawled. "The duration and nature of your services will be in accordance with the Goverments instructions. Ah Ahem! Your pay will continue until your arrival back in the United Kingdom, subject to your giving satisfactory services. Your travelling expenses will be paid and you will have first class passage to the East, and, Ahem, you will have five minutes to think it over. It's to take over these German steamers," he added.

"But", said a prospective candidate to this venture, "according to that agreement we might be kept in the East indefinitly, and if we don't know the nature of our services, how can we know our services are likely to be satisfactory?"

"The agreement is not a cross word puzzle, I refuse to argue. To me it is perfectly plain!" said the agent coldly. "If you wish to join the venture kindly sign here, if not, let the next gentleman …"."

"The next gentleman ai'nt going", said a man with a high life nose and a nautical appearance, "at least not unless there's some cash advance," he added.

"I say! Look here, confound it", said the agent crossly, "it's my conviction that…"

"That's all right", said the nautical one, "I never read police reports, and another thing I would'nt be seen in this office again".

"Unfortunately you would," sneers the agent. "Yes my dear fellow sign here, and this is your order for medical examination, your ticket and passport will be forwarded with your instructions. Goodday."

"Well, that's that." I thought as I made for the surgery in Commercial road for medical examination.

I find the place and join some other patients in the waiting room. It is to be a long wait; the doctor has been called away urgently and can't see anyone until later in the evening. I pass my medical examination and miss my train home, but it's no use complaining.

It is only a short time since I left the oil tanker after a ten-month voyage and now this, but men must work and women must sleep, usually after they have seen their husbands off on the early morning train. My alarm clock fails and I almost miss mine. I just have time to tell my wife to be good and to read her Bible every day, particularly the gospel according to Saint Mark, verses 35 to 38.

There has been a strike on the railways and porters are as scarce as old maids in Turkey. It makes little difference, for neither porters nor taxi drivers like the look of my battered and heavy old sea chest that has not been used since my apprenticeship days and is now covered with labels saying 'Glass', 'Eggs', and 'Fragile'. Large luggage is the bane of travel; I don't mind the lighter stuff if the cork can be kept in.

I have the compartment to myself on leaving Waterloo station. The train is actually on the move when in comes a couple of suitcases followed by a balding and shabbily dressed clerk-type person. He sits down opposite me and within a few minutes has presented me with his business card, introduced himself as Marmaduke, and accepted my offer of a gargle by pouring a good two-finger nip from my flask into a glass produced, apparently, from his hat. Marmaduke claims to be a lieutenant in the Royal Naval Reserve (RNR), has been awarded the Distinguished Service Order (DSO), and is desperate to return to the East again. He has already realised that I am one of the party. 'You stick to me, George,' he says. 'I've had years on the China coast and the river boats. It takes some time to know the Chinaman.' He then tells me that the Chinese shipowner treats you infinitely better than the creatures owning vessels at home and that no one in London knows what nightlife is really like unless they have visited Shanghai.

'A rickshaw out to the Lung Whao Pagoda, a dinner of the "Pudding of the Eight Precious Things", a little music, perhaps a little smoke,' he confides in me quietly, 'every sin the experts have learned in seven centuries can be found if you know where to look.'

The train arrives at Southampton and 150 different ranking members of this mercantile marine expedition are on the platform with a mountain of luggage. Apparently no arrangements have been made for dealing with us, yet many are in excellent spirits. Eventually, motor lorries are chartered and our gear is taken down to the cross-Channel boat.

The wharf and the packet boat are deserted except for a supercilious army officer rapping out orders that no one takes but the slightest notice of. It is raining and there are no porters, so the masters, mates, and engineers have to carry their own baggage on board, although not without some pointed remarks as to the ultimate destination for a certain government department.

A general move is made towards the naval paymaster's office. Many of us have practically no money and now is the time to be securing some travelling expenses in advance. The courteous, yet very worried, paymaster has great difficulty in understanding why no one has considered obtaining a banker's draft that could be cashed at various stopping off places during our long journey.

'An excellent idea,' agrees Marmaduke who, like me, has only a few pounds with which to get to Singapore. 'Several people handle my affairs, but mostly J. Walker and Co, they are so safe you know. And who might be your bankers, George?' he asks quite loudly.

'I was known at the bank of Loch Lomond,' I say, 'but…'

'Gentlemen,' shouts the paymaster above the babble, 'I am authorised to advance you £1 each, and that is all.'

'Then this is as far as I go,' bellows another voice, 'what about my train fare back home?'

At this point, Marmaduke thinks it a good idea that we abandon our quest for money and go ashore to a hostel he knows where we can take a drink and talk further about our financial matters. We talk a lot further than intended and forget that the boat is meant to sail at midnight. Luck is with us, however; for some unknown reason she doesn't sail until the early hours of the morning.

At noon the next day we are chasing a harassed 'Cooks' agent around the quay in Le Havre. The poor chap has his work cut out trying to organise this crowd. About three-dozen cabs arrive to take us to various hotels to await the night train for Paris. A portion of my small capital vanishes in the hotel when my new overcoat, hip flask, and my cap are removed from the hotel hat stand. I have to travel to the Gare de Norde station to catch the 'pink' train, or whatever they call it, in a large black felt hat and an ancient cloak that have been left as gifts by the person who obviously found my coat and hat to be better than his own.

We arrive at Paris in the early hours of the morning and, unlike being in England at this time of day, are able to quickly find a nice café. One must be gay for one's first trip to Paris, so after breakfast I am wrapped in the arms of Morpheus on the hotel lounge sofa until it is time to proceed on the next step of the journey. A few of our men manage to see the sights; they even bring them to the station to say goodbye!

I distinctly told Marmaduke to keep a lookout for me at the Paris Gare de Lyon station, but there is no sign of him. I collect both our 'luncheon baskets' that a thoughtful governmental department has provided for us through the Cook's agency, find our luggage, and secure corner seats on the Marseilles express before searching once more for Marmaduke. I spot him talking to some Americans officers at the buffet. 'Come along Marmaduke, I've been searching Paris for you, there's only five minutes left. The gear is on the train and I've got us corner seats.' Three minutes later a worried looking Marmaduke is dashing along the platform, obviously taking heed of my warning that he would miss the train.

'Here we are,' I say, leaning out of the window, 'a carriage to ourselves and-'

'What the devil are you doing in there?' he yells. 'You fool, you're in the wrong train. Where's our luggage?'

The French porters are such idiots: they have put me and our baggage on the wrong train. We just have time to cross the platform. The express is on the move as our gear is thrown in followed by us. I think it careless of Marmaduke to sit on my cardboard lunch box and reduce the contents to a mixed salad. He makes up for his error by hurling what remains of the box through the open carriage window straight into the face of a silly grinning porter. 'If the Ministry can't supply us with a better lunch than that, then we shall have to dine on this,' he says, producing from his bag a bottle of cognac that restores us to a less peevish frame of mind.

At Lyon some of our men are missing, including a fellow to whom Marmaduke had lent 50 francs. They had been seated in the front portion of the train, which hadn't been destined for Marseilles.

We join an old Pacific Mail liner in Marseilles; she had been a good vessel in her day, which was a long time ago. Instead of sailing at once as expected, we have to wait ten days for 2,000 Chinese workers – who are being repatriated to their home country – to embark as deck passengers. With that number on board, the outlook for us cabin passengers is not so pleasant.

The delay in pushing off allows us to visit Marseilles. The trams dash along the dock road regardless of people or other traffic. One morning the tram in which we are riding to town scatters a crowd of dirty and villainous-looking Turks waiting to board a steamer. One unlucky man is knocked down; fortunately, the pink feather mattress he was carrying on his shoulder acts as a buffer, although he seems displeased at seeing his new mattress lying in the mud. A little further up the road we collide with a cotton-laden wagon and every glass pane on the port side of the tram is broken. A cotton bale hits me in the back, throwing me into the arms of a pretty young widow sitting opposite. A baby feeding on the breast still complacently takes its nourishment despite the uproar. Marmaduke is all for making a claim for shock, but receives no support because no one can understand English.

Selling his sextant for a good price enables Marmaduke and me to finance a French lifestyle of sitting in a café and making one drink last for a couple of hours. The café we prefer has music and is located in the Rue de Cannebierre,[i] a fine street with an abominable cobblestone surface. Popular with the locals, it is generally full to overflowing with all kinds of people: working men with their wives and families, business men, French sailors, decorated and pompous French military officers with their rows of medals, British officers and nurses, and a plentiful sprinkling of professional ladies. The hum of conversation typically rises and falls like waves on a beach.

The hanging around waiting for the ship to sail doesn't suit either of us and eventually we are forced into seeing the sights. We visit the cathedral, the Palais Longchamp, and even manage to take a nap one afternoon on the soft turf in the grounds of the zoo. Marmaduke decides our sightseeing should extend to a stroll around the slums of Marseilles. This is not a safe pastime by any means; we enter some dreadful dives and are lucky in not being molested.

We take to strolling along the magnificent breakwater in the evenings before dinner. Before turning in at night, I have to hang up my shirt that has very bright and different coloured stripes so that Marmaduke, who is sharing my cabin, can determine the state of his health in the morning. If he sees that the stripes have run together when he wakes up, he knows he should only be drinking plain soda for the day. The Eastern way of life has touched his liver.

We leave Marseilles with the 2,000 Chinese people bedded down all over the decks. After being at sea for less than 24 hours we suddenly find our cabin is occupied by two Greeks and our gear has been put out into the alleyway. We recapture the cabin and throw out their stuff, but a little later the ship's captain is apologising to us and saying we must vacate the cabin as the Greeks are very important personages. Many of our party make a great row about this, but we have to get out just the same and end up sleeping in hammocks along with a dozen other men for whom cabins cannot be found.

We are surrounded by the deck passengers. I can tell you confidentially that our lives become very uncomfortable and unhygienic, especially with the temperature rising by the mile. Many of these passengers have gramophones that are played 24 hours a day; the continuous Chinese music sounds just like a series of dog fights.

When we arrive at Port Said, a strong letter of protest about the conditions of this first-class passage we were promised in our agreement is sent ashore to the Duty Naval Transport Officer. Some underling nincompoop comes on board and reports that the 'accommodation is as good as that for repatriated Australian troops'. It is the same old tale: officers of the merchant service are deliberately swindled and yet we have no redress. One or two of the single men throw their hands in there and then and demand their passage back home.

At Colombo, there is a rush to get ashore. Stepping into the streets of this city brings it home that we have arrived in the East, and a very nice East it is too. The trees are in full bloom and heavy with a gorgeous scent as the rickshaw bowls us along the smooth road out to the racecourse. It is fortunate that we have a few drinks at the Bristol Hotel before the meeting starts. The horses do not run at all as hoped and at the end of the racing we are without funds but badly in need of a drink. Marmaduke seems unperturbed by our lack of finances and enters a curio shop and asks to see some expensive rubies. In a moment, chairs, cigars, and two cold beers are placed before us whilst Marmaduke, looking suitably impressive, carefully inspects the rubies through a small magnifying glass. In spite of being given more free beer, he fails to find a stone quite good enough to please him; we walk out of the shop and make our way back on board.

All is in uproar after the ship arrives in Singapore and is moored in Keppel harbour. In the saloon an agent is examining passports and giving out tickets with the names of the various hotels at which we are to stop. By luck, we are amongst the first in the queue. Marmaduke, being at home here and knowing the ropes, is in his element. 'How much money have you got left, George?' he asks. 'I have nothing left at all myself!'

'Two shillings is my total,' I say dolefully.

'That's alright, let's have it quick,' he demands before turning to a Chinese porter he seems to know. 'Hey there, Yet Sing, get all this luggage down the gangway and into the cart for the Adelphi.'[ii]

Singapore being a free port, there are no searches by Customs to delay us in getting away from the ship. In a few moments our gear is on a bullock wagon, and we are bowling along Robinson Road in a smart little two-horse gharry.[iii] We are stony broke and without a smoke, but Marmaduke is at ease. 'Quite alright now dear boy,' he assures me, 'our worries are over for a time. We are bound for the Adelphi Hotel and I am known there.' We look prosperous enough in our spotless white uniforms, newly pipe-clayed shoes, and topees, but with arriving in what to me is a strange eastern port, I would have felt more comfortable had I just a little cash in my pocket.

Marmaduke strolls into the Adelphi. 'We want one of your best rooms facing the cathedral,' he says to the proprietor, 'and you can pay the gharry, I have no small change. Also, send a couple of bottles of whisky, a box of the best cheroots and a couple of hundred State Express cigarettes up to our room.'

We are conducted to a fine airy room facing St. Andrew's Cathedral[iv] with its pleasant green turf grounds. Marmaduke instructs the bellboy to fetch two 'stengahs' – iced whisky and soda – whilst we move onto the balcony to look down into the street.

'There you are, George, now you can see the reason for the hurry. Here come the stragglers, they won't get a room like this and they won't receive the attention that we did. You have to be first in the field in this game.'

We were indeed just in time! Marmaduke had been wiser on this occasion than he could ever have thought. The next day the agents issue a warning throughout the city that they will not hold themselves responsible for any debts we contract, and advising tradesmen of all kinds to ask for cash on the nail. This is bad news, very bad news, for in the East when a white man's chits are stopped he loses status amongst the servants and the local people in general. However, in fairness to the agents, I am afraid that under the circumstances it is the wisest course for them to take, for otherwise it is very likely that bad debts would be contracted all over the city.

Most people live for years in the East without touching a penny in actual cash. Everything is bought by simply signing a chit. You may think that tradesmen are taking considerable risks, but with the practice extending throughout the whole of the East, there are very few bad debts. A man is immediately placed in an unfavourable position when his chits are no longer accepted.

We stay in the Adelphi on full pay for two months with the Government paying the hotel bill of £1 per day for each of us. Whilst the living is excellent, the lack of money causes the usual trouble. I can tell you that the white man living ashore in the East with little or no money to spend has a pretty thin time of it. For hours Marmaduke and I, a handsome pair of that there is no doubt, just sit in vain in the hotel café outside looking into our empty glasses in the hopes that someone will come along and fill them.

There is a weekly excursion to the agents to get whatever cash advance they will permit; this amounts to very little for a married second officer leaving half his pay or more to his family. If he is to have any pocket money at all, he must wash his own clothes in the hotel bathroom, which is a dreadful thing to have to do when staying in a first-class Eastern hotel.

Singapore lies 77 miles north of the equator and has a population of nearly 303,000; about 70% are Chinese, many of whom are millionaires. The climate, considering the nearness of the equator, is mild, and English children are said to thrive in it. The gateway to and from the East, it is the third largest port in the world based on the amount of shipping that passes through it. Passengers transship here for Australia and other ports in the Far East. The outer roads are always crowded with large vessels at anchor and the inner harbour is packed with coastal steamers and native craft.

The Botanical Gardens[v] are lovely, the vegetation ranging from European to impenetrable African jungle. There are several English churches in the city, and five important street markets. Raffles Museum, with its splendidly preserved great gorillas in fighting attitudes and the tigers shot by the Sultan of Johore, is well worth seeing. There is a very fine park, which is the country seat for the Governor of Singapore.

Although Marmaduke doesn't care much for walking, we agree it's no good hanging around the hotel with very little funds. One must get some exercise in the tropics to keep fit. We decide to wander around the town before heading out into the country to the Sea View Hotel[vi] to see if we can cadge a drink or two from some of our party who are staying there.

We pass over Cavenagh Bridge[vii] which crosses a narrow and nasty-smelling river crowded with as many junks and native craft as the Regent's Canal Dock has barges. These boats are home for fowls and other livestock that have been reared on board as well as thousands of Chinese people, many of whom have never set foot on shore.

Rather than spending the last of our money on a rickshaw, we stop off at the Hotel Europe[viii] to have a stengah. This is one of the finest hotels in Singapore and I fancy their whisky to be better than elsewhere. Further up the road from the Europe is the well-known Raffles Hotel,[ix] which registers about 60,000 guests a year and is owned by the immensely wealthy Sarkies brothers from Armenia. The Savoy of the city, it has its own post and telegraph office, a grill, and an American bar. Marmaduke, who has stayed there, says it isn't up to much, but I know their ice creams are the best in the city.

We pass through the Japanese quarter, which is presently under boycott by the Chinese, before reaching the distinctive-smelling Chinatown. It is Saturday afternoon and the roadway is crowded with stalls and long trestle tables where remarkable dishes are being handed round to hungry Chinese men clad only in their comfortable sarongs. Everyone seems to be placid and happy with no quarrelling or drunkenness, and with half the noise to be heard in Deptford High Street on a Saturday.

Here are stalls selling multi-coloured drinks, dried-up looking cakes, evil-smelling fish, and rows of little dried carcasses that Marmaduke says are rats. We see the plaintive satay seller with his wares in two baskets on a bamboo pole; the white-clothed, bareheaded, pot-bellied Hindu usurer; the Tamil labourer with stick-like legs; the bread seller; and the snake charmer. We pass a joss house, looking restful and exactly the opposite of the dingy abominations the English call Chinese temples or shrines, and yet we are sending out money that has been collected by passing round the hat in our tin Baptist chapels to convert these so-called heathens!

Beyond the market place are the Chinese workshops, every trade having its own little colony. The tradesmen are as busy as bees in their dark and mysterious little shops, using much the same tools that were being used centuries ago. There are quaint sailmaker's stores; goldsmiths crouching low over their tables, pausing in their work only to give us a swift glance over their big horn-rimmed spectacles; cedar wood workers; tailors; and rattan chair and basket workers. Huddled together in a tiny workshop, you can find 20 Chinese men all working at great speed, while the little naked children play in the roadway regardless of the continual stream of motors.

It is said to take more than a motor car to kill a Chinese child. When one does get knocked down, the tall brown Bengali policeman will swear long and loud at the child and its parents instead of taking the motorist's name and number. He will curse them for several generations for not having more care. The heathen mother will carry the child indoors before returning to the spot with paper and joss sticks to kneel down in the highway and pray that the evil spirit may be either chased from the roadway or from her child. She burns the paper and lights the joss sticks, and the child's clothes, if there are any, are held towards the sun. This is a busy street, but whilst this is going on all the traffic, including the rickshaws, is suspended. It all seems a bit silly to me, but there is no sign of any annoyance. If a British mother should start kneeling and praying in the Strand after her child had been knocked down, she would be 'run in' if not run down first.

We now pass the shipbuilding yards where the excellent Chinese carpenters continue with the centuries-old tradition of building their junks entirely from wood and with dowel pegs being used instead of nails. As we move into the open country and through a coconut plantation, the bullock wagons mingle more with the traffic. It is about a five-mile walk from the city before we reach the Sea View Hotel.

On our return from the hotel, we pass a Chinese wedding party with the bride inside one of the many gaily coloured sedan chairs. It must be a rather costly business; money is being thrown to the large crowd that follows the procession to the deafening din of tom-toms, cymbals, and firecrackers.

To relieve the boredom, I take up writing. There are two or three newspapers printed in Singapore and they seem to be rather hard up for news; they must have been for they accepted an article from me!

After two months of loafing around, I receive a ticket for some place in New Guinea, but this fell through and was changed for Padang in Sumatra, via Batavia. And very much via Batavia, it turned out to be. I say my farewells to Marmaduke; he has been a good friend.

Koninklijke Pakketvaart-Maatshappij,[x] a Dutch shipping company, has the monopoly of the passenger trade to the Dutch East Indies. The service from the Javanese stewards on board this company's vessel is very poor; perhaps they have twigged the shortage of guilders amongst our contingent, or perhaps it is the ordinary standard of service, but whichever, I am extremely lucky. For some unknown reason I am given the seat on the top table next to the captain of the vessel so all my meals are warm and served at least half an hour in advance of the rest of the crew. I learn very quickly how much these Dutch captains can eat!

The vessel calls in at a couple of small ports before proceeding east of the Thousand Islands to Tanjong Priock, the port for Batavia, an artificial harbour costing £1.5 million to build. We arrive in Java, the Pearl of the Orient, and from what I hear it seems likely we will remain on this island for some time. The temperature is about 80°F all year round (no frozen water pipes) with the month of October being the unhealthiest period as that is when the monsoons change.

We are stowed away in a number of German motor cars and are driven by utterly reckless Malays to the hotel Weltevreden Batavia, which is situated in the well-planned and well-built modern part of the city. The hotel is a large rambling series of bungalows with all of the buildings only one storey high on account of the earthquakes. The whole length of Java, some 570 miles, is a part of the great volcanic band that runs from Sumatra to the Philippines.

The thick whitewashed walls and the stone floors keep the bedrooms fairly cool. The wardrobe in my room is full of ladies underwear, but the American commercial

impudence to land over an inch thick onto his spotless decks; the ashes were still falling when the yacht was 300 miles away from the island.

A little later in the same year, another eruption took place of such a terrible nature that the coastline for many miles on both sides of the Sunda Straits was completely devastated and thousands of people lost their lives. A remarkable disturbance of the sea occurred in various parts of the world on the same day. In some places the pumice lay many feet thick upon the sea surface, giving the appearance that the ocean bed had suddenly risen above the water.

Steam from the volcano was estimated to have risen to a height of 12 miles in the air, and a rain of ash fell over all Sumatra. Finer particles of dust floating in the atmosphere enveloped the earth and caused the most brilliant sunsets up to December of that year. The sound of the explosion was heard in Perth, Western Australia, New Guinea, Ceylon, and Mauritius. The tidal wave off Batavia rose to 72 feet. I read that the volcano on Krakatoa erupted again in 1928[xviii] and that the island has now disappeared altogether.

The ship drifts through the Banka Straits where the shore looks to be more or less impenetrable jungle, past Singkep and the Lingga Islands and through into the Singapore roads. For over two months the vessel lies at anchor waiting for a turn in the dry dock. Ex-German steamers are coming into this port from all parts of the East and before they can proceed on their voyages, they must all be docked.

In the dry dock, a wonderful display of marine growth is attached to the ship's bottom; there are barnacles and oyster shells as big as plates. The steel of the hull has been eaten clean through in places, so thousands of rivets are required to make her seaworthy. Forty Chinese labourers die through eating the oysters found on the hull, the paint and rust having poisoned them.

The climate is so humid that one's clothes and boots would be thick with green mould within a week without any brushing or attention. The insects play utter havoc with all our woollen underclothes and socks for which, of course, we receive no compensation.

One of the worst features of this trip is the total disregard of the Singapore agents for the mail sent out to us from home. Weeks go by without any mail being received, which causes the greatest discontent. Afterwards it was found that our letters had been in the agents' office all the time, including important registered mail for myself which, by the way, was returned to me from their office some six years later. This non-delivery of mail was disgraceful. The consequences of withholding these letters can sometimes be very bad and far-reaching.

I have now spent only six days at sea as second officer in the seven months I have been away from home, which must make it a very expensive business for the Government. The cost of refitting this ship alone has run into thousands of pounds, and our ship is only one of hundreds. The taking over of the German mercantile marine was probably a costly mistake.

In Keppel harbour we load a very general cargo for Marseilles, Rotterdam, and London, consisting of copra, rubber, coffee, pepper, coconut oil, citronella oil, ore, tapioca, gambier,[xix] tin bar, sago gum, green peas, shellac, tortoiseshell, and with a few more commodities loaded at Penang and in other ports.

Off Socotra, a fire is discovered in the hold containing 1,000 tons of copra, the dried shell of the coconut. Once this oily stuff gets well alight the usual methods of combating fire are next to useless. Being a German ship there is an excellent firefighting system that involves piping steam from the main boilers into any compartment of the vessel. If it hadn't been for this, the ship might well have been in a bad way.

The copra is still burning away when we reach Aden. The only way to put the fire out is to completely flood the hold, but what a ghastly mess. What was left of the cargo in the adjoining hold is badly damaged by the terrific heat; imagine hundreds of bags of half roasted coffee, rubber that has been melted, and so on. The damaged cargo is unloaded and spread about the beach in Aden, partly auctioned off, and a little re-shipped after the holds have been scraped clean and painted.

The best time to visit Aden is at dawn and to leave during the same dawn if at all possible. I hope for your own sake that you don't know Aden. There's no trouble with frozen water pipes and over busy plumbers here because the only water in the place is that which has been distilled, and in any case, no one wants to drink water in Aden. I think it only rains once in every hundred years or so. The Romans built great water tanks cut into the rock with a collection system so that should it ever rain, the water will run into the stone reservoirs. I went along with the third mate to view these tanks; someone told us that they are supposed to be the only thing of interest in Aden.

The ship lies off these barren rocks for about six weeks. There is little to do for the navigating officer once the damaged cargo has been discharged, so I go for many a solitary sail in the gig exploring the local coastline. I think the other officers believe me to be mad, but I don't feel the heat so much with my topee and umbrella. I don't come to any harm, although I must say there are many cooler places than Aden at midday.

Homeward bound, we pass through the Strait of Messina and more volcanoes. The southern part of the strait lies almost under the shadow of Mount Etna, which is about 87 miles in circumference and 10,880 feet in height. In the rising sunlight of dawn, the snow-clad smoking peak is painted in gold, rose, and purple colours that make it look a good deal more beautiful than no doubt it really is.

Coming from the south, the land is closed about a mile from the beach at Cape Spartivento. From there to Capo dell'Armi at the south-eastern entrance to the straits, the countryside is composed of high-rolling and down-like hills descending steeply to a golden sandy shore. The sun plays on the vivid green of the pastures and lights up the reddish-browns of the moorlands, the purple and yellow heather, the white buildings of scattered villages and solitary farms, the moving flocks of sheep far up the green hillside, and the gleam of many watercourses winding their way through the valleys to the sea.

The lighthouse at Capo dell'Armi is like some feudal castle perched on a towering and precipitous cliff. The tide comes boiling and swirling down the channel, a billion diamonds in a turquoise setting; it was on account of these strong and irregular currents that these straits were so much dreaded in ancient times. Peculiar tide rips and whirlpools along with changeable and violent gusts of wind rushing down from the mountain gorges made navigation of sailing craft in these waters a difficult matter. By keeping very close to the Italian shore when the tide is running to the south, the ship will get the counter-current running to the north; the dividing line between these two streams can be plainly seen.

At Reggio, you may see the mail train pulling out from the brilliantly coloured railway station that is built almost on the beach. Two large black engines give a final whistle and the train is away, winding its way along the golden shore and rumbling over low bridges. Lost for a moment behind the white buildings of some village, it gives another peep before being swallowed up into the mouth of a tunnel that stands out vividly in the face of a large white cliff.

A large double-funnelled ferry boat passes us close, bound for Messina opposite Reggio. Here we bear over to the western shore and pass the town of Catania which is situated on a flat stretch of land jutting out into the sea. This area suffered terribly in the violent earthquake of 1908 when 97,000 lives were lost and Messina and Reggio were destroyed. Mount Etna erupted again in November 1928[xx] causing considerable damage.

It pays every traveller and ship's officer to have a really good pair of prism binoculars. I have a little pair made by Ross and Co that fit easily in the pocket but are as powerful as a large marine telescope. I have spent many interesting hours on ship's bridges with them.

Shortly after leaving the straits, we can see the purple outlines of the Lipari Islands with the active volcano of Stromboli smoking angrily away in the distance. Stromboli is about five square miles; the volcano is in a state of continuous eruption, emitting flames and vapour and yet the people persist in living on the island. They grow their wheat, currants, and raisins and tend to their vines that, in spite of the eruptions, produce some of the finest wine in the Mediterranean. In July 1921 the volcano erupted violently and several lives were lost.

After discharging the last of the cargo in London, the vessel went up to the Tyne for extensive repairs. She then loads 6,000 tons of hay for El Qantara military camp in the Suez Canal before proceeding out to the Far East to load a full cargo of 11,000 tons of rice for London. The vessel is then sent up to the Tyne again where she is laid up ready for sale, and all hands are discharged.

Paying off the vessel doesn't sound particularly tragic, but it is the start of a period of terrible unemployment for members of the mercantile marine that is to continue for the next few years. I need to tell you about these things in the hopes that you will understand the situation more clearly.

The captain of the vessel was never one given to talking ship's business with his officers, yet at the end of that voyage he called me to his cabin and privately showed me his own account of wages. His total earnings amounted to just a fraction more than the wages of the cook. I am afraid the landsman will find it hard to realise quite what this means. My friend the chief officer, an RNR Lieutenant Commander with a very distinguished war service, received wages for the whole voyage, which were just the same amount as the young second steward. The reason for this is that the Cooks and Stewards Union demanded and got overtime payments for their members. The master and officers have no union, hence the result.

Anyway, the ship is to be sold; I later hear that the Germans bought her back after all our trouble and expense. It is not only this ship that is laid up for sale; over 400 ex-German ships are sold in England and their crews rendered unemployed, with very little chance indeed of them getting more work for a long time to come. With 2.5 million tons of British shipping lying idle, it is almost useless to look for employment, particularly as an officer:

> I want to say right here that the un-employment in the mercantile marine has
> been just as bad as the coal miners in 1928, and yet it was not broadcast, oh

proposed partnership would make a good business. Five months later the farmer was declared bankrupt with no assets and liabilities of thousands of pounds!

Eventually I find a man who wants to borrow money on the security of his stock, and who will engage me as a cowman and general labourer at a good weekly wage, although a good wage in agricultural terms means next to nothing! I am also to have a half-share in the farmhouse.

We journey to the place in a Ford van piled high with our gear. The cat has kittens en route, the parrot shrieks curses in Spanish as to the coldness of the passage, and we can't get to the farm without a tow from a horse. And then we find some of our furniture is too large to go in through the door. The frame of the upstairs sitting room window had to be taken out and the piano and other items hoisted up and through the opening with the help of a tackle.

The farmhouse is typical of Sussex, with white weatherboards almost to the ground and a heavy stone slab roof. All the old oak beams are plastered over with whitewash and the bedroom floor slopes a couple of feet from the door to the window. Our bed has a collection of bricks under the legs. Our sitting room resembles the cabin of a ship that has been laid up for some years; it is long and low, so low that what is left of the plaster comes down in showers when we bump our heads on the ceiling.

These old Sussex farmhouses are all very well in summer, except for there being no bathroom or proper sanitary arrangements. In winter though, with the cold stone slab floors, the draughty doors and windows, the rats biting the babies' toes in bed, and the hundredweight stone slabs falling from the roof during the winter gales, it can all prove rather trying.

The farm itself is not a prosperous one for otherwise I wouldn't be here. It has only 45 acres, but another 40 acres is rented from a neighbour. The soil is mainly heavy Sussex clay, which is one of the trickiest soils to work. In the summer drought its surface becomes as hard as iron with great cracks two or three feet deep upon which not even the strongest of agricultural implements can make the slightest impression. In heavy rain the land becomes a morass with great clay clods the size of a football sticking to one's feet. Such a place is a continual struggle to make ends meet, unless the farm is merely being used for pleasure.

We have nine cows of which six to seven are in milk at any one time, the milk being sent away daily by train to London. There are a couple of yearling heifers, a sow with her litter to be reared for porkers, a few calves, and about a score of hungry-looking, but non-laying, barn door fowls. Two heavy horses are used for operating the farm implements; Old Tom is not only old and very bad tempered, but also hates the hay rake. Of course the place is understocked, but given the present drought and falling prices, it happens to be quite fortunate.

The position regarding farm implements seems much the same as most smallholdings trying to carry on with insufficient capital; the tools and harness are mostly second-hand and more or less held together with string. What we don't own we borrow, and hours are wasted at the most critical of times making hasty repairs.

For labour there is the farmer, his son – who doesn't like farm work – and me. Very occasionally outside help is employed at harvest time. To anyone who wants a spell of really hard manual labour, I would recommend them working on a hard up and understaffed smallholding. The average deckhand at sea would collapse entirely if he had to do half the work that a man does here. I'm afraid none of this sounds either too promising or romantic. It certainly isn't, and it doesn't fall in with the idea of a 'dear old farm' in the slightest.

(I could tell you a very different tale of a Devonshire farm, a place where money didn't altogether matter. What a contrast, for money makes all the difference in the world of farming, as in most other walks of life. There I rode hunters for exercise along lovely flower decked lanes and my work, although often hard, was on the free and easy lines with shooting, playing bridge and very pleasant outings. It was only in Devonshire that I have seen the 'jolly old farmer type'; most of the farmers in this part of the country appear to be pale-faced and harassed looking individuals.)

Here there are 101 jobs that all want doing urgently and at once. The work is hard, yet there are compensations. There is nothing quite like walking behind straining horses with their jingling plough tackle turning up the sweet-smelling brown earth on a bright spring morning; seeing the distant daisy-sprinkled pastures and hedgerows fragrant with wild primroses and daffodils; smelling the scent of the cow stall at milking time; feeling the warm soft skin of the beast as she waits to be milked; or hearing both the hiss of the milk as it squirts into the pail and the plaintive cry of the hungry calf waiting outside.

Sometimes such work seems very worthwhile, but not in financial terms. A ploughman can walk nine miles in a day behind a 200 lb. plough; feed his horses a full hour before taking them out; groom and feed the horses again when the skilled and heavy work is done, and get paid five shillings[i] or so a day for the pleasure, and with that he has to keep his family.

The lack of modern machinery is a great handicap on this farm. For chaff and root cutting, we have only a very antediluvian roundabout affair that is powered by

11 A HAULAGE CONTRACTOR

A haulage contractor is my next venture; why this is so I really cannot say, since I know nothing whatsoever about the business. In some vague way I must have thought of all the years I've spent transporting goods at sea, and then asked myself, why not on land? A sensible argument, as you will no doubt agree. In just a few months I shift all kinds of things, including all my capital.

We have a problem of no house. We have nowhere to go on leaving the farm, and houses to rent are as scarce as emeralds in this part of the country. The sales manager who wishes to sell me the motor lorry can wangle a cottage for us to rent providing I buy the machine from him. There is also a motor driver who, by taking him into partnership, can find me plenty of work. I do both.

The motor lorry is a 40 horsepower affair all painted for the occasion. The big portable canvas hood for furniture removals is extra, as is the polished wood-framed windscreen fitted with plate glass and the big gas-fired headlamp – an utterly useless object. The garage gives me a six-month guarantee and promises to thoroughly overhaul the lorry and have it completely ready for the commencement of my first contract. It is looking a grand turnout.

Our cottage could be worse. It's in a lovely situation facing an estate of wild and neglected woodland bristling with pheasants and free firewood, although a bucket must be thrown into the bowels of the earth to obtain fresh water, and the sanitary arrangements are not of the modern labour-saving type. The water from this community well has some strange properties; strangers coming here have wondered if they have contracted dysentery and babies cannot drink the stuff at all.

I missed making a fortune through a complete lack of initiative. If I had only sold the lorry for half the price I had paid for it and invested the money in medicine bottles, printing, and advertising, I might by now have owned a Rolls Royce and a fur coat. The only risk to the venture would have been the well running dry. I would have had labels printed along these lines:

> It is better to give than receive. This wonderful aperient remedy
> is a combination of natural salts and human ingenuity.
> Discovered by that brilliant post-war young man, Captain Bones,
> M.B.B.A. after years of hard and patient research, it is sold to
> the public at so low a price as to be unparalled (sic) in the history
> of medicine. This unique remedy can be obtained at 2/3d per
> bottle post free from the Natural Springs Laboritories.(sic)

The truth lies in the bottom of the well, along with the dead cat and the wedding ring belonging to the lady next door. I seem to remember retrieving the body of the cat!

The motor lorry looks a bonny machine the morning we go into the country town to fetch it from the works. There is the manager, beaming and rubbing his hands, as well he might in dealing with such a jay as me. I am told I will receive 'the best of attention at all times' and to bring it back if anything should go wrong. 'What's that sir, there's no petrol in the tank. George, fill up the gentleman's tank with No.1, that's the only spirit we stock, sir, and that will be two pounds, six shillings and eight pence please, sir.' I notice there is no toolbox. 'No tools, sir. I'm sorry, just an oversight, sir. George, please get the gentleman a set of tools. There we are, sir. I'm sure you'll do well. Goodbye!'

We have been underway for about a mile when an explosion occurs in the engine room that brings us up all standing. The fan blades have come unstuck, ripping the guards off the radiator and damaging a tube, which leaks continuously after that. The only thing to do is to proceed slowly and park the machine in the shed I have hired for a garage in the yard of the village pub.

The fan is repaired the next day and we set off to commence a contract of carting into the market town some 200 tons of cordwood that had been stacked by the roadside in a remote country district. Before we have gone a couple of miles, away goes the fan again, raising a dent in the engine cover the size of a plum pudding. With the ignition switch broken and the petrol pipe leaking so badly that it doesn't need Sherlock Holmes to track our passage, we head back to the works where they decide I had better leave the machine for a day or two to recuperate. Then they smooth me over with a drink or two!

It takes 23 days to complete that wood carting with the lorry back in dock for several days under repair. The petrol consumption is outstanding; a couple of gallons go as quickly as a thirsty stevedore's first pint. Cordwood is supposed to be logs of not more than four feet in length, but underneath the pile we find great trunks of oak weighing several hundredweights that need extra labour and a tackle to get them on board the lorry. We have no redress because the word 'cord' has not been mentioned in my written contract, which is a dead loss.

I have been 'done' on my first job, but at least the countryside around here is lovely. It is October and the apple-picking season; we can buy a whole sack full of windfalls for a shilling and take them home in the lorry.

Various charters follow the wood carting, but all at freights too low to give any profit after taking the running costs of the machine into consideration. The enormous petrol bill swallows everything.

We have cargoes of brick rubble, ashes, manure, hay, and a few furniture removal jobs, if one can call the sticks owned by the unfortunate people who have been evicted furniture. I can't leave them and their stuff stuck out in the lane, although I must say that probably anyone but a crazy seaman would have done so. The 12 shillings I charge doesn't even cover the cost of the petrol. The song says 'I am a bizineth man', but I don't really think so!

The next job is a good one; we wash as much of the manure out of the lorry as we can, buy a few bales of straw, tie some green baize around our middles, and proceed to a big seaside town to move furniture from the top flat in a lofty house out into the country. Nothing in the flat has been packed; pictures still hang on the walls, the breakfast dishes lie on the table, and the lady's undies are in a heap on the bedroom floor. She is a cheery soul; we have a glass of port together and discuss how very unhelpful some furniture removal men can be.

'But you don't mind it upside down, do you?' she asks.

'Certainly not, my dear madam, I like it like that!'

She won't accept a lift back with the lorry, insisting that she travels by train instead. Unfortunately she catches the wrong one; it is nearly midnight before she arrives at her new quarters. Still very cheery, she pays up all right, and tries to kiss me!

I find that attending farm sales and markets in the hopes of finding work is of no use. Backing between market stalls of flowers and cheap alarm clocks, and with cattle rushing about all over the place is not suitable work for a machine such as this lumbering great pantechnicon.

During the first week of 1922 a little man who had heard I wanted a helper appears at the cottage door. He refuses to acknowledge that business is so bad that employing more labour is out of the question and insists upon touting for work with some of my business cards. In a few hours he is back with quite a few contracts. I have to write most of them off at once, apologising to the customers for the mistake in the costings, but even after raising the prices we get some of the work.

In the month of January one gets a good idea of what prehistoric Sussex must have been really like. The valleys at the foot of the Downs and other districts of this Weald country are flooded, not entirely without benefit to us because we can stop now and then to wash the lorry down.

The roads and lanes are in a fearful state for a heavily laden vehicle. With one cargo of coal we are delivering to a farm, I draw to the nearside of the lane to allow a two-seater to pass. With the eight-ton weight on its edge, the side of the ditch collapses. Going astern only made matters worse. We light the riding lights and go home. Next day, I charter a horse and cart to deliver the coal, another loss for the business.

We also make a loss on a job carting mandrels from the railway station up a lane to a farmyard that resembles a quagmire. We get up the morass and alongside the barn, but after unloading most of the mandrels we find that the wheels are stuck in the mud. Trying to back out is disastrous; the whole machine sinks up to the back axle.

It is impossible to jack her up without a solid foundation. After several hours, we place timber under the wheels and chains around the tyres, and cut a roadway. I put her full astern and with one bound our work has been lost and she is more deeply in the mud than before. Even in this remote spot the usual crowd has mysteriously gathered.

'Try 'er once again, Governor.' I do so. What an engine! This time she leaps like a steeplechaser straight out of the hole. 'Don't stop her,' yell the crowd. I don't; with the helm hard-a-starboard, she shaves past the trees and a nearby haystack. Like a battle tank in action, she crashes through the rotten fencing at the bottom of the field and out into the lane where she pulls up, trembling like a leaf. I get out and sooth her down; one must use kindness, even with a motor lorry engine!

In winter the work is very hard. We start off one bitter snowy morning at 5 a.m. from the middle of Sussex to go to the wilds of Kent and a remote village somewhere near Canterbury. It is just the weather to suit the lorry engine, for once warmed up she settles down to a deep roar and eats up the snow-covered roads across Chailey

Common. By 8 a.m. we are having hot rum in a pub on Hadlow Down.[i] Outside Ashford we run aground in a snowdrift for a couple of hours. The weather becomes worse, the heavy snow blots out our landmarks, and we lose our course completely. The landlord of a pub near Barham Down puts us right and by 3 p.m. we make our destination. We have travelled 90 miles, not bad going considering the heavy weather conditions!

If we made a good passage outwards, then the homeward journey easily eclipses it. The charabanc man who had told me of this job drives and we average 18 miles an hour for six hours despite being unable to see the slippery and twisting roads with the useless gas headlamp flickering on and off. The lorry is a clumsy pantechnicon, not a Hispano-Suiza, and to steam 190 miles in 21 hours with many stops for refreshment and loading is good going.

It is said the Romans were good road makers; they employed men of less than 80 years of age and fixed the time and length of meal hours. This 'patching' of the main roads they are doing at present is terrible. A few old men – when they are not sitting by the roadside eating – scrape some tarmac about, throw some sand on it, and leave us overtaxed heavy haulage people to roll it down. There are infinitely better roads in the Dutch East Indies and in the Malay States than the main roads in England, and that shouldn't be the case when our roads are carrying a hundred times more traffic.

A newspaper states: 'The greatest highways of Great Britain are being built today. Few of us know where it is going to end.' I don't believe we do; it's not in Sussex anyway. Perhaps we are waiting for another Mr Macadam, who did for our drivers much the same as Mr Plimsoll did for our seamen, and got the same thanks!

I meet a real old woodsman who would travel 20 miles to do a hard day's work felling trees and then cycle 20 miles back home afterwards on his dilapidated old tricycle; a man fond of work, beer, and driving a hard bargain. He can't stand motor vehicles unless it is one like mine that hauls his wood at a very cheap rate. He had been cutting down a coppice, nothing too serious, just the undergrowth of a complete wood. The man would have made a good stevedore for he loads the lorry with 75 great bundles of pea boughs and 800 clothes props, all consigned to Brighton. Our course is through the ancient seaport of Steyning, which will later calmly nestle miles inland under the Downs. It is a lovely drive with the cool sweet breeze mingling with the petrol fumes until the cursed machine comes to a standstill; a valve in the engine has gone terribly wrong. I am faced with yet another repair bill.

One of my main jobs is brick haulage across the beautiful Surrey Downs to a lunatic asylum near Epsom[ii] where I think they will have me as an inmate if I keep the job for much longer. Alas, driving 100 miles a day five days a week and 50 miles on Saturdays is proving too much for me; I have to flood my own carburettor too often to carry it on. My route takes me across Holmwood Common where one can see gypsies, herds of wandering cattle, and the monument to the late Mr Vanderbilt[iii] of coaching fame.

Like most of us I envy the gypsies in the summertime; a mysterious people foolish enough to prefer the country to the city slum, who could pass like noisy shadows into the lonely spaces and broad expanses of the countryside. Regarded by the 'respectable' townsman as thieves and clothes peg-selling nuisances, these gypsies have more respect for other people's property than many a prosperous company promoter. It is mainly game or garden produce they steal, and that ruins no one, and when they do raid the hedgerows, it is only the ferns and the wildflowers that suffer from their depredations. I wonder how small a proportion of the community really cares about such things.

The van of one couple I met was painted a brilliant chocolate, blue, and yellow with a touch of flaming vermilion; with its brightly polished brass, it brought to mind a continental barge. Two years later when master of a little barge, I met these people again in the Sloop Inn[iv.] in St. Ives, Cornwall. They were still roaming the countryside and remembered me at once.

We have a bit of lorry trouble outside the White Hart Hotel in Dorking and again at the Burford Bridge Hotel after crossing the little bridge spanning the River Mole close to where the great elms overhang the road. With a full cargo of bricks on board, I realise the brakes aren't quite holding her as we go down the steep hill to the main road leading towards Leatherhead. I have little choice but to take the right-angled turn into the main road and ignore what is coming along the other way, for otherwise we will be in the White Hart Hotel regardless of opening hours!

I am sorry if you're not familiar with some of these places, but at least we all know Epsom and the Derby races. The Captain Cuttle Derby[v] – what a day out! My friend, the poultry dealer and an awfully nice chap, drove me in his Ford van free of charge and with some free refreshments if I would sit beside him and play the banjo for the crowd behind to sing along to. I'm not a racing man to describe the Derby. All I know is that when Steve showed his head around the 'corner'[vi] all was blotted out and there was nothing more to see. The canvas hood of the van upon which we, and several other impudent and uninvited persons had been standing, had collapsed!

I take a job hauling 20,000 bricks from some very isolated brick works to an 'isolation' hospital. The very sound of the place should have been a warning, besides which it is too far from our base to return home at night.

There is particularly bad weather in the month of March 1923. There is snow about and the Surrey countryside is a quagmire. The first view of the hospital, which perches on top of a hill as steep as a roof of a house, reveals I have taken on something out of the ordinary. How the fully loaded lorry manages to get up that hill is a marvel. They say these Peerless engines[vii] are renowned for their pulling power during the war, but this proves it! She pants and puffs up that slope using a gallon of petrol for every couple of hundred yards, whilst my assistant walks behind with a baulk of timber in case she goes astern.

On getting back to the brickworks we have to look for lodgings. I drive to the only houses for miles around, a small row of dilapidated looking cottages. With a half-a-crown bribe in his palm, the old labourer, who had been standing at the gate of his cottage, says he will see what can be done; we wait in the garden for the verdict.

It came through the open window in a plaintive old voice. 'Oh dear, oh dear! Send 'em away, send 'em off, I don't like the look of 'em.' The old man has never been in a motor before so I drive him to the nearest pub. An hour later he is quite sure that we should lodge with him. Peace is made with the poor old wife through the medium of stout and, of course, my charming manner. She shakes like jelly with some nervous complaint. 'Oh dear, oh dear. Girls had to work in my young days,' she tells us, '14 hours a day in the fields for a few pence. I could do as much as any man then, but now I can't even cook for you. All I can do is just sit here and shake, oh dear.'

The interior of their picturesque thatched cottage is horrible, falling to pieces with no proper fireplace or ventilation and with tiny fixed windows, and yet the old couple has to pay several shillings a week rent. It goes to show that even when one is old and very poor there's no kindness or chivalry in this world.

It takes a couple of 12-hour days with no stops for meals to shift 9,000 of these confounded bricks; we get to loathe the sight of them. Then our luck runs out once again. On the last journey of the day, in the dark and in the blinding snow of a blizzard, all the packing blows out from the engine's hot water jacket. We come to a halt in a lonely lane a couple of miles from the nearest inn, where we manage to get a room for the night. In the morning, having cleared a foot of snow from the machine and after applying some putty, two handkerchiefs, and some very hard words, I manage to get it to a garage. With repairs made, we complete the job at the end of the week. When we leave the cottage the old shaking lady cries and kisses me!

When we stayed the one night at the inn we got hold of a furniture removal job, the only time we ever had a breakage in this work. It was for an elderly spinster of a rather suspicious nature, who stood at the door to watch every article entering her house. To our horror we discovered the breakage. One of a pair of bedroom toilet-ware articles was broken; we were lucky it wasn't one of the stuffed cats in glass cases, although from their looks it should have been. I dared not tell her, so my assistant carried in the unbroken article, carried the same one back out again wrapped in straw, and then carried it back in a second time to make an unbroken pair!

I never had an accident while driving this lorry. The nearest I came to having one occurred when I was going for a load of sand and had my wife and children, and another lady and her offspring, with me for a bit of a picnic. An old horse in the shafts of an ancient gig suddenly ran right across my bows. There was no time to pull up so the only thing for it was the ditch. At the side of the road in that spot was a large pile of road-mending stones, which I mounted. The lorry took a great list to starboard before coming back down again into the clear road, so on we went, but it was a very near thing.

I think the isolation hospital brick job put off my helper. When we are at Brighton a little later with another load of pea sticks, he vanishes completely together with three two-gallon cans of petrol and some tools. The best of luck to him; he was a good little worker and a positively wonderful beer drinker!

My next assistant is a horse breaker. We help each other in our respective jobs, but there isn't much work going on in either. The lorry continually gives nothing but trouble: if it isn't a broken valve, it is the pump, or one of the chains. I go to the auction marts in London to try to sell it, but the country is overrun with old war stock and they are practically giving lorries away. Shipping is just as bad as ever. We are becoming very hard up, so we decide to try something new.

In a field by the side of a main road crossing, we put up the canvas hood from the lorry to act as a tent, fly a few old flags, display an old white enamel cask painted with a sign 'Home-made Lemonade' across it, and set up as ice cream merchants with a borrowed freezer. A jolly good paying game it is. We do a great trade while the bank holiday lasts. My signpost attracted some attention, and not all of it positive:

An elderly military type gentleman pulls up in his car alongside the sign.

"Try our ices, sir?"

"Ice cream be damned, sir. What is the meaning of this outrage?" pointing to my nice sign.

"Joe," I said, "what is the meaning of this outrage?"

"Don't know, looks like a motor car," says Joe, my partner.

"Have a glass of genuine home-made lemonade," says Joe.

"Curse the lemonade Sir, if I had my way I would place you under arrest!"

"Yes, we could do with a rest, very busy, wonderful Ices, you don't know what you're missing."

"I will report you to the police Sir," says the Major, or perhaps General, driving off.

I decide to do no more haulage work, but just as I lock up the shed, a lady offers me a tempting job at my own price, which I purposely make high. I have to cart 30,000 old bricks from a farm to a well-known country mansion. I do one day's work before every cog comes off the differential gear; the repair costs £25 and I conclude that luck is no longer with me.

Bought at an exorbitant price, the machine has never gone as it should. My petrol bill[viii] for the short time I have been at work is well over £100, and there is a bill as long as a towrope from the firm who sold me the lorry under guarantee. It has long been a scandal that garages pretend to repair imaginary defects in cars and bill for work that has never been done. Knowing that I've been cheated, I make a stand with their last bill, but things are becoming too bad. I stow the lorry away in a quiet backyard near Brighton and say goodbye. She has taken us some thousand miles and I've looked after her in health and sickness, mostly the latter, for several months.

A ruined man financially, I join a ship in Cardiff later that evening. We are pretty well broke and my boots are leaking.

Left: The author, probably
at Swandean Hospital

Below: West Africa – the
author being offered the
choice of the 'King's'
three daughters for an
evening's 'entertainment'

Above: Newport News – Horses of all
shapes and sizes ready for loading

Right: Newport News – under the
re-fuelling coal trips/chutes

Top: Horses corralled in horseboxes on board
the horse transport

Above left: The author posing with a
telescope on the deck of the horse transport

Above right: The author next to a horsebox
on board the horse transport

Left: Newport News -
loading horses

Lower left: The line of
horseboxes on board

Lower right: Newport
News - loading horses

Below: A plan of the 'paravane', a confounded contraption

Lower: The convoy leaving Milford Haven

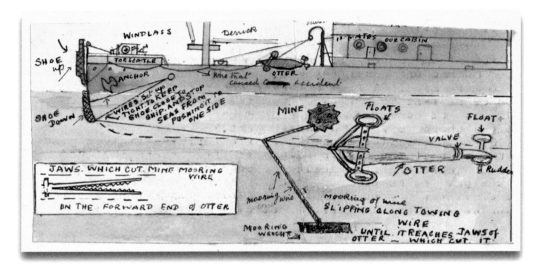

Left: A schematic map of the Suez Canal

Upper right: A scene in the Suez Canal

Middle: a ship in the Suez Canal, viewed from ashore

Lower right: Passing a sailing ship in Suez Bay

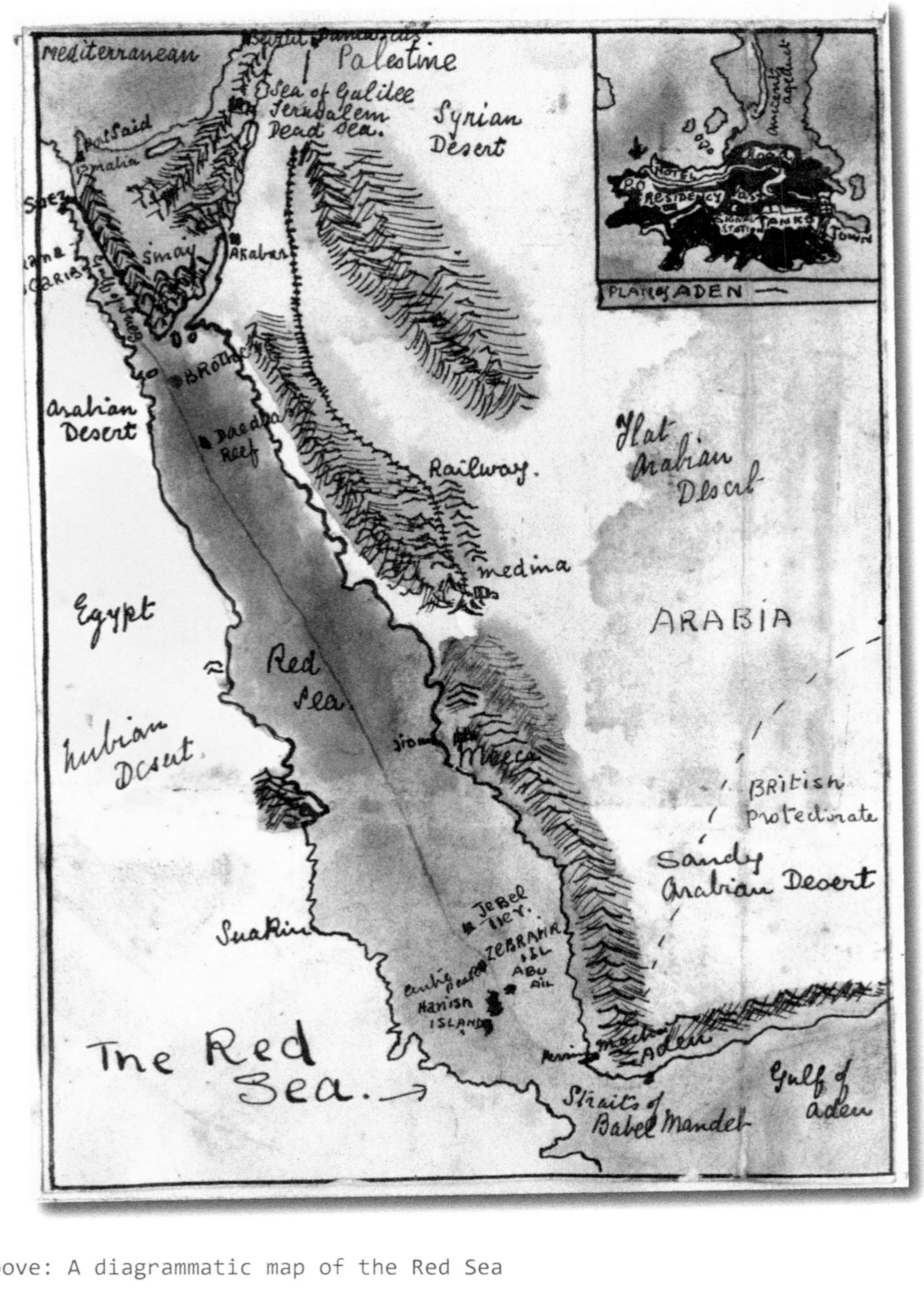
Mediterranean
Palestine
Sea of Galilee
Jerusalem
Dead Sea
Syrian Desert
Port Said
Suez
Sinai
Akabah
Brothers
Arabian Desert
Daedalus Reef
Railway
Flat Arabian Desert
medina
Egypt
ARABIA
Red Sea
Nubian Desert
Mecca
BRITISH protectorate
Sandy Arabian Desert
Suakin
ZEBRAHIR ISL
ABU AIL
HANISH ISLAND
Aden
The Red Sea.
Straits of Babel Mandeb
Gulf of aden
PLAN of ADEN
HOTEL
RESIDENCY
TANKS
TOWN

Above: A diagrammatic map of the Red Sea

[Opposite page, three lower images]

Upper: ‘Zaffarana lighthouse’ (Ras Zafarana), Red Sea

Middle: ‘Ras Gharib lighthouse’, Red Sea

Lower: ‘Daedlas shoal’ (Daedalus Reef/Shoal), Red Sea

On the Suez Canal

Port. Rock. Light. House

Upper: Transiting the Suez Canal

Above, left: Newport Rock lighthouse (Suez)

Above, right: 'Peculiar formation of hills
in the Red Sea' (author's description)

Zaffarana. Light. House

Daedlus. Shoal.

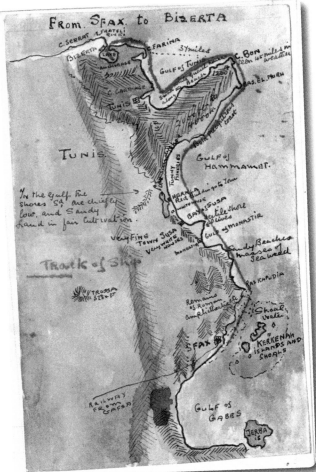

Above: Loading phosphate rock at Sfax in Tunisia

Left: Diagrammatic map showing the ship's track from Sfax to Bizerte

Left: A hand-drawn map of the Mexican oil ports

Right: Tuxpan – the shore pipeline from the ocean bed

Below: 'Entrance to Victoria', Brazil

East Coast of Mexico

Tampico

Railway

Cape Rojas

Lobos Island

Dangerous Reefs

Tuxpam Bar

Gulf of Mexico

oil pipe line

sand dunes

Cazones

Mt Orizaba 18206 feet

Penote Mtd 13400

Wild mountainous coast

Vera cruz

hilly scrub

Cordyz cobbers road

Porto Mexico

disused Railway

Railway to Mexico city

O Rizaba Town

Salvia Cruz

Pacific Ocean.

Prairie

ENTRANCE TO VICTORIA. BRAZIL.

Left: 'A Monastry at Victoria' – possibly the Penha Convent

Below: 'The Goal at Victoria'

Below: Rio de Janeiro, Copacabana beach

Upper: Rio de Janeiro, Sugar Loaf mountain

Above: The *San Gregario* in Rio de Janeiro. The author has drawn the two other tankers he later commanded, for size comparison

Right: Impression of Rio de Janeiro at night

LEAVING THE SUGAR LOAF ASTERN
NIGHT IMPRESSION OF RIO JANERIO

Above: Santos harbour approaches

Top right: The old Fort Santos

Right: Moella Island

Above: It doesn't matter what's your colour in Rio de Janerio

Right: 'A nurse girl, aged 9, in Santos'

Far right: Loading coffee in Santos – the weight on his shoulders is 302 kilos

[Opposite page] A hand-drawn map of the Brazillian coast

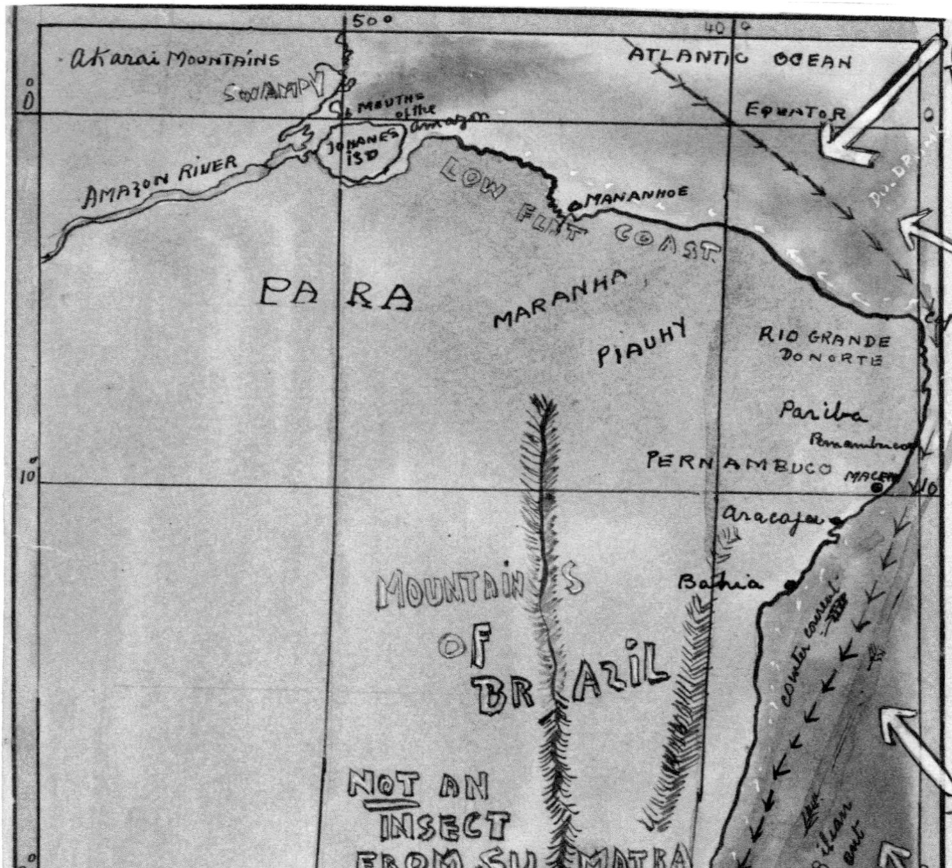
50°
40°
Akarai Mountains
SWAMPY
Mouths of the Amazon
JOHANES ISD
AMAZON RIVER
ATLANTIC OCEAN
EQUATOR
NE TRADE WIND
SE TRADES
LOW FLAT COAST
MANANHOE
PARA
MARANHA
PIAUHY
RIO GRANDE DO NORTE
Cape San Roque
Pariba
Pernambuco
PERNAMBUCO
MACEIO
Aracaja
Bahia
MOUNTAINS OF BRAZIL
NOT AN INSECT FROM SUMATRA
counter current
Brazilian current
SE TRADE WIND
SE TRADE
VICTORIA
Cape St Thom
Cape Frio
RIO JANEIRO
SANTOS
OUTWARD
SAO. PAULO
DESTERO
TO PARAGUAY
0 100 200 300 400
ENGLISH MILES
VARIABLE WINDS
TO MONTIVIDEO

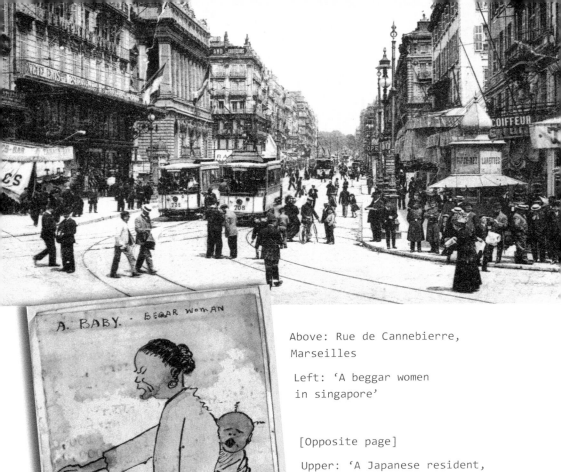

Above: Rue de Cannebierre, Marseilles

Left: 'A beggar women in singapore'

[Opposite page]

Upper: 'A Japanese resident, a motor accident and a refreshment stop for a rickshaw driver, Singapore'

Lower: Quai de Belges – the waterfront – Marseilles

MOTOR ACCIDENTS
ARE FREQUENT

Modern
JAPAN
IN
SINGAPORE

DALHOUSIE OBELISQUE

STATUE TO KING OF SIAM

A PRINCIPAL OBJECT
OF INTEREST

Top: By the Post Office, Singapore

Right: The Waterfront, Singapore

Below: The Europe Hotel, Singapore (demolished in 1935)

[Opposite page]

Upper: The different types of people in Singapore

Lower: 'Native craft on the river', Singapore

Upper: The canal in Batavia, Java

Middle: Native women washing their clothes in the canal, Batavia, Java

Lower: A bungalow on a rubber estate, Java

A railway bridge between Batavia and Tjimahi, Java

Commencing the mountain climb by rail, Batavia to Tjimahi, Java

Upper: The harbour at Bencoolen (now Bengkulu)

Above: Fort Marlborough, Bencoolen

Right: The author on his trip to view the Roman water tanks in Aden

[Opposite page] A detailed hand-drawn plan of the 45 acre farm in which the author purchased a share

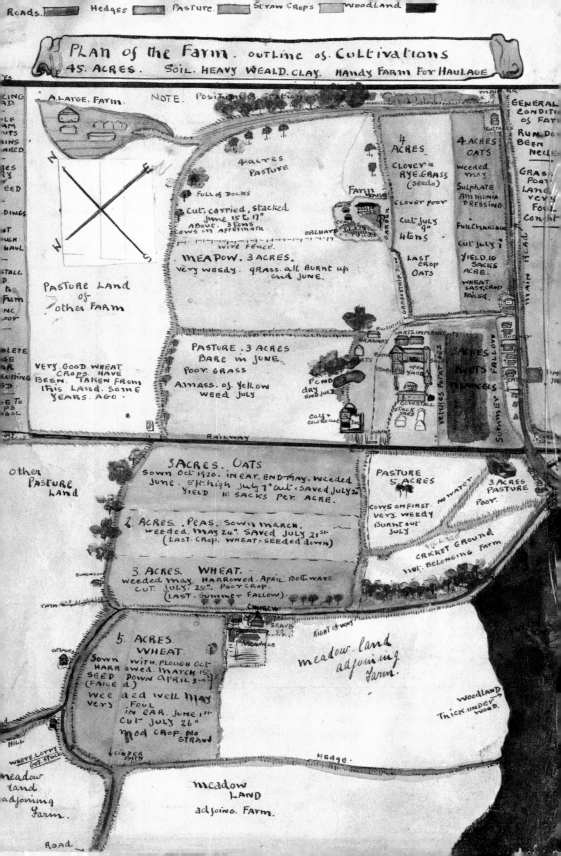

Roads [____] Hedges [____] Pasture [____] Straw Crops [____] Woodland [____]

PLAN of the Farm. Outline of Cultivations
45. ACRES. SOIL. HEAVY WEALD. CLAY. HANDY FARM FOR HAULAGE

A. LARGE. FARM. NOTE. Position of station

GENERAL CONDITION OF FAT...
RUN DO... BEEN NEGLE...
GRASS POOR LAND VERY FOUL CON...

PASTURE LAND of other FARM

VERY GOOD WHEAT CROPS. HAVE BEEN. TAKEN FROM this LAND. SOME YEARS. AGO.

4 ACRES PASTURE
FULL OF DOCKS
Cut, carried, stacked June 15 to 17"
About 3 Tons COWS ON AFTERMATH
WIRE FENCE.
MEADOW. 3 ACRES.
VERY WEEDY. GRASS ALL BURNT UP END JUNE.

FARM HOUSE
ORCHARD

4 ACRES
CLOVER & RYE GRASS (SEEDS)
CLOVER POOR
Cut JULY 9"
4 TONS
LAST CROP OATS

4 ACRES OATS
WEEDED MAY
SULPHATE AMMONIA DRESSING
FULL CHARLOCK
CUT JULY 7
YIELD 10 SACKS ACRE.
WHEAT LAST CROP FAILED

PASTURE. 3 ACRES
BARE IN JUNE.
POOR GRASS
A MASS. OF YELLOW WEED JULY

GRANARY OATS
CARTS. IMPLEMENTS
OPEN YARD
COW STALL
STACK YARD
CALF & COW HOUSE

3 ACRES ROOTS
MANGELS
VETCHES POTATOES
SUMMER FALLOW

POND DRY END JULY

RAILWAY

Other PASTURE LAND

3 ACRES. OATS
Sown Oct 1920. IN EAR. END MAY. WEEDED June. 5ft. high JULY 7" Cut & SAVED JULY 26
YIELD 10 SACKS PER ACRE.

2. ACRES. PEAS. SOWN MARCH.
WEEDED. MAY 24" SAVED JULY 21st
(LAST. CROP. WHEAT. SEEDED DOWN)

3. ACRES. WHEAT.
WEEDED MAY. HARROWED. APRIL. BOTH WAYS
CUT. JULY 25" POOR CROP.
(LAST. SUMMER FALLOW)

PASTURE 5. ACRES
COWS ON FIRST. VERY. WEEDY
BURNT OUT JULY

NO WATER

3 ACRES PASTURE
POOR.

VILLAGE CRICKET GROUND
NOT. BELONGING FARM.

5. ACRES. WHEAT
Sown WITH PLOUGH OCT
HARROWED. MARCH 15
SEED DOWN APRIL 3rd (FAILED)
WEEDED WELL MAY
VERY FOUL IN EAR. JUNE 1ST
CUT JULY 26"
MOD CROP. NO STRAW

BUNGALOW
CHURCH
VICARAGE
GRAVE
RIGHT OF WAY

meadow land adjoining Farm.

WOODLAND THICK UNDER WOOD.

COTTAGE
WHERE LORRY GOT STUCK
HILL
CINDER PATH

HEDGE.

meadow land adjoining Farm.

meadow LAND adjoining FARM.

ROAD

Left: The children — Anitra on the left, and either John or Gerald on the right

Below: The 40 horsepower lorry purchased by the author in his failed attempt to become a haulage contractor

Left: Flooded roads in January 1922

Above: 'Helm hard-a-starboard, she shaves past the trees and a nearby haystack'

Lower left: 'Like a battle tank in action, she crashes through the rotten fencing'

Above: The *Doresetshire* moored at Wallaroo jetty in January 1923. The four masted barque, the *Marlborough Hill* is moored on the opposite side

Left: The Glasgow Puffer under the author's command

Lower left: The outer harbour, Peel, Isle of Man (1923)

Right: The inner harbour, Peel, Isle of Man (1923)

Right: Peel Castle viewed from the headland

Below: Lizard Head and the lighthouse

Lower: The author (on the port side of the open wheelhouse) as master of the *Ben Robinson* (note his dog positioned in front of him)

Above: Penzance harbour

Below: Land's End and the Longships lighthouse (on the left)

Above: Longships lighthouse (on the right) and Whitesand Bay

Below: St. Michael harbour, (St. Michael's Mount), Cornwall

Right: Sunset on the cornish coast

Above: The *Ben Johnson* in high seas off the Longships

Left: Faversham, where repairs to the *Ben Johnson* were carried out

Centre left: Believed to be Faversham

Lower left: A Thames sailing barge, unkown location

ON THE upper REACHES
of the THAMES.

GLN.

Above: Scenes on the upper reaches of the River Thames

Right: Herring gutters at Peterhead

Below: Tiers of ships laid up on the River Tyne, North Shields

Top: Peterhead viewed from the harbour

Above: Peterhead gaol and the breakwater

Below: Entrance to Aberdeen harbour in rough weather

Above: Aberdeen Harbour

Below: Alderney harbour showing the road into the town in the foreground

Above: The Coaster's Saturday night

Right: The author in second
officer's uniform, date unkown

Left: The author's
funeral expenses
– dated 2nd
December 1929. The
executors of his
estate paid the
funeral director's
invoice on 18th
March 1930

12   To Australia as Quartermaster

It is not very pleasant after sailing for so many years as an officer to be running about in a sailor's round hat and blue jersey as a quartermaster, a term used on liners and the best class of cargo vessels for the man who steers the ship.

The ship[i] is a fine 10,000-ton vessel with a diesel engine, the latest thing in marine technology. The engine room has an appallingly complicated appearance with a mass of electrical machinery for working the steering gear, windlass, and cargo winches. The initial cost of such vessels is very high, but the saving in fuel is very great. There are, of course, no firemen, but a staff of nine fully certified engineers and two electricians.

The Lascar[ii] crew are berthed right aft in the modern cruiser stern that affords considerable extra space. The accommodation for the four quartermasters is also aft with two men to a room; the cabins are well fitted and comfortable with a large bathroom adjoining. This accommodation is significantly better than that provided for the officers on board the majority of large tramp cargo steamers.

A galley boy brings our meals and cleans our cabins. The food is excellent and so abundant that every day enough to feed a large family in plenty is thrown overboard from the quartermasters' mess alone. For various reasons, it isn't the policy to return it to the galley; in any case, it would still go over the side.

The very fact that a ship such as this should be loading coal shows the state of shipping, for in normal times she would carry nothing but general cargo; it is like a commissionaire at Harrods standing at the door touting for custom.

Whilst passing out of the dock, I was standing with a fender on the main deck when I noticed the Lascar seamen on the poop jabbering and pointing at me. A man rushed down, grabbed the fender from my hand and saluted. The native bosun's mate, or *tindal* as they are called in their own Hindi language, had sailed with me when I was second officer on the ex-German liner and he seemed much upset to see me fallen from the ranks of the mighty. These Lascars take this kind of thing to their hearts if they like you; I couldn't have agreed with them more!

A quartermaster's work is fairly easy if somewhat monotonous. Two men are on watch at a time and we keep four-hour watches, four hours on and four hours off. At 4 a.m. one of the two men going on duty takes the ship's wheel and steers until 6 a.m. when his mate, who has been cleaning the wheelhouse and the bridge brass work, relieves him. After having a smoke, the man who has been steering finishes the cleaning work. At 8 a.m. these men are relieved by the other pair coming on watch, one of whom goes to the ship's wheel while the other does some canvas sewing work or repairs the flags. The process is repeated from noon to 4 p.m. The 'dog-watches' are from 4 p.m. until 8 p.m. when the steering is shared between the four men to change the watch hours, so that the pair who had the eight-hour duty the previous night now have the eight-hour watch below. In port, one quartermaster always keeps watch on the ship's gangway, whilst the other men work at keeping the navigation bridge in order.

The vessel goes to Hamburg to load some ironwork; it's just my luck being short of money. I'm working off my month's advance in wages, or the 'dead horse' as we call it. Here in Hamburg everything is very cheap for us with an armful of German marks[iii] being given for a one pound note. Our voyage from Hamburg to India takes us through the Bay of Biscay and the Mediterranean towards Port Said and our crossing of the desert into the Red Sea. My skills and patience as a quartermaster are severely tested in the narrow waterway:

> The ship does not steer at all well with this electrical gear, the French pilot on the Suez canal gets very excited which is nothing uncommon. "Ah quartermaster, you steer very good, eh? Port a leetle, Steady. Ah bon, a leetle more port quartermaster. Ah, ah. What is ze mattaire. Port, port. Sacre, Mine God. Hard over ze helm. Hell Godam. Ah steady, bon. Zat is good. Alright quartermaster, bon."
>
> What with all the officers, cadets and red tape on a ship like this, the officer of an under staffed old tramp would be wondering what the blazes was the matter.

Bombay is an imposing looking city when viewed from the sea with glittering domes and all the rest of it. The railway station is said to be the finest building of its kind in the world. The usual crowd of silk sellers, fortune tellers, toenail trimmers, tailors, cobblers, and curio merchants hang around our quarters all day.

The large Sailors' Mission arranges a temperance trip for the cadets; although I don't particularly want to spend the money, I have to get off the ship for a break and to drive around with the boys. We go by launch to Elephanta Island[iv] to visit the famous ancient caves. There are carved Buddha figures umpteen years old that are of great interest, but half of them are missing where the sand has fallen away. It is very hot with lemonade the only stimulant handed round, but some of the boys sample the 'holy water' against the keeper's orders. We have our photos taken, but there always seems something wanting on these missionary outings!

The ship completes discharging at Rangoon and we have our Christmas dinner of 1923 on deck in the blazing sunshine off the north-west coast of Australia.

We anchor off Port Pirie on a soft and mellow January evening. The night skies in the Spencer Gulf are punctured with a million lights from the white streak of Orion to the Southern Cross, beneath which the town lights twinkle. A gentle warm breeze ripples the surface of this almost landlocked harbour as a half-moon rises over the smudge of the distant hills. At home my wife is probably struggling to hoist some icy well water and in Canada… Why people should want to go there when South Australia exists, I simply don't know!

Our loading berth is opposite the Barrier Hotel, which is a little too close for comfort in this hot weather and when funds are low. Port Pirie is quite a nice little town with good American-style shops with soda fountains in the drugstores and so on. All the shops and saloons close sharp at 6 p.m. and don't open on Sundays.

The cost of living is not dear, wages are much better than in England, and there is no unemployment to speak of. A small four-roomed wooden bungalow rents for around ten shillings per week with board and lodging for a working man costing about 30 shillings a week. A good deal of labour is employed in the large and evil-smelling smelting works that produces about 1,000 tons of lead and zinc concentrates a day, with the unskilled workers being paid 12 shillings per day. The average daily pay for carpenters and for the stevedores loading wheat in sacks into the ships is £1, and that is for an eight-hour day and not a minute longer.

Sailors on Australian coasting vessels are paid £11 per month with their food included for an eight-hour day with a day off for every Sunday spent at sea. As far back as 1872, the well-known author Mr Frank T. Bullen[v] wrote:

> The wages of Australian seamen were £7 per month and 1/6d per hour overtime. Firemens wages were £10 per month. The best of food was provided, and many of these men owned house property on shore.

It makes you think a bit! Compare that with the mere pittance and the vile food doled out to British seamen of that period, and then look at the conditions and wages for British seamen in 1923. As a quartermaster, my wages are £9 per month for a 12-hour working day, and there are no holidays for Sundays at sea.

Whilst the ship is loading the bagged wheat, the quartermasters are stationed in the holds to see the mats are properly spread to protect the sacks from the ironwork of the ship's structure. The stevedores are a pretty tough crowd; Swedes and Dutch predominate in Port Pirie with many of the population being deserters from the windjammers. They are very independent people and portray a total lack of servility, but they seem mild enough to me when compared with some of the dockers from Poplar or Deptford on a good day. One man of the stevedoring gang does nothing for the complete shift but go across the road to keep the petrol cans filled with beer.

The finishing port for loading is further down the Gulf of Spencer at Wallaroo, a very pleasant little port with a long woodpile jetty extending far out into the green waters of the bay. In the evenings and on Sundays the jetty is used as a promenade by the community who, like most Australians, take a kind and sympathetic interest in British ships and sailors. On Sunday afternoon people come from far and wide to see the big motor ship and soon the vessel is swarming with interested visitors and many pretty girls. Some of our cheap curios change hands at a nice profit. Strangers invite us to their homes for tea – imagine British people asking the crew of an Australian vessel in the London docks to visit their homes! Some Londoners don't even know that the docks exist!

At Wallaroo the men loading the wheat are paid 22/6d[vi] per day, but when the shipping season is over there is not so much going on in the port. The majority of stevedores have small farms and come down every day in their buggies or Fords. There is very good fishing off the jetty; fish of strange shapes and unusual colours can be seen far down in the sparkling green water. As many big fat crabs as one could possibly want can be caught by dropping an easily made trap net baited with a piece of meat onto the sea bottom.

On the opposite side of the jetty to us lies the old four-masted barque, the *Marlborough Hill*.[vii] I can remember her from my apprentice days, but for some years now the Russians have owned her, and she looks it! She is manned mainly by

Finns with a big German skipper, and what stories she could tell of the last 40 years. She is loaded with wheat and is waiting for a few dropouts to be sent round from Adelaide to make up her crew. A few days later she looks a fine sight as she squares away to the south on her long voyage to Falmouth.

My fellow quartermasters and I have a whole Sunday off to go bathing by the splendid beaches. The firm hard sand stretches away for miles, shoaling gradually so there is not too much surf in the deliciously warm water. The cobalt sky and the white sun-bleached dunes form a beautiful backdrop to the golden sand. From the blue-black offing the sea turns a lighter shade of green until it meets the snowy surf. Away to port lies the old jetty; a white schooner rolls lazily at her anchorage and the small gulls quarrel and shriek. One can remain for hours in the water and then lie and smoke on the balmy sand until the sea turns a sheet of silver and the sky becomes a great blotch of scarlet and saffron with a steel blue background.

The air is full of ozone and the nights are soft and beautiful. Parties drive down to the beach, switch on their headlights, and go bathing until midnight. Sharks do not often come into the shoal water; there is a special bathing pool for children and the nervous near the town.

Some of the cargo is loaded from small auxiliary schooners that collect the grain from the small ports in the Gulf. I get to know the skipper of one beamy little craft that carried about 130 tons with an eight-foot draught. She is schooner rigged and can make a speed of five knots under sail and her diesel engine. A small four horsepower paraffin engine on deck powers the cargo winch used for discharging and also the winches for the anchor and for handling the sails. The skipper's home is in Adelaide where, he told me, there are no slums and no poor people.

It is 1923, and there is a good deal of fruit-growing and wine-making going on up the Murray River. They say there are going to be great developments in the region. I only wish I was in a position to stop out here and make the most of them:

> In the district round here wheat farms stretch away to the Broken Hill mines, a good workman gets £4 per week on these farms. At the mines thousands are employed, miners pay being 33/0 per day, an unskilled trucker getting 17/0 per day. Whatever job you take on in South Australia you must become a Union member. Unions (many of them) in Australia, are not the silly, futile, capitalistic run, affairs they are in England. They are a very powerful weapon of self defence to the worker. When they strike – and unfortunately, strike seems the only means to keep up wages and conditions, a fact obvious to a child, else why are the conditions so much better in Australia than in England.

Every man I questioned, and I made it my business to get all the information I possibly could, all seemed satisfied with their work and pay. They like the country. How many farm workers, clerks, sailors, and what not, would you meet in England to day, who would say the same. Very few! If it can be done in Australia it might be done in England, but not with the get-rich-quick-at-any-cost type of employer about.

It's a big subject, too big for me, yet this I do know, that the market for mercantile marine officers was deliberately flooded after the war in order that the supply should far exceed the demand. There is only one reply to that game, a reply that officers of the merchant service, thinking of their own people and the population in general, cannot give. I hear people babble of the 'General Strike' there never was a general strike. So long as the 'Jugular Vein' of the country, so long as the most vitally important industry we have still kept going smoothly on, then, how can there be a 'general strike'. You don't believe it? Well I tell you, when the mercantile marine stops work, then the fireworks will begin. We can do without most things at a push, but Jolly old Reader, take it from one who knows we can't do without the mercantile marine for a week.

That's my opinion! I am not a Socialist, a Communist, or a Bolshie. I grab anything that comes in reach of my long skinny fingers, so I'm Conservative, and if I had the chance would be as big a rogue and thief as any capitalist you could mention. Anyway what's it all matter?

On sailing day the Lascar cook is missing. To leave a coloured man behind in Australia means a heavy fine for the ship. Unlike the shipping companies that have employed thousands of Lascars and Chinese to take the place of British seamen in the mercantile marine, there's no place for them in Australia.

We have a monotonous 40-day passage to Naples ahead of us. At the entrance to the Spencer Gulf we pass the *Marlborough Hill*. She has been a week at sea and has sailed only 130 miles.

From off Cape Leeuwin we have a clear run of 5,000 miles to the African coast. When the very small amount of fuel used is taken into consideration, the driving of 15,000 tons deadweight through the water for 30 days without a stop at a speed of 11 knots is a wonderful achievement for these diesel engines.

Naples would disappoint any tourist the morning the ship arrives. There is a nasty and cold misty rain, and what can be seen of Vesuvius looks sad and forbidding. I find Naples to be a queer place. Bands of wandering musicians with mandolins and guitars come on board to play for our leftovers of food. We even hire an orchestra to play in the quartermaster's mess at mealtimes for our scraps. I am the man stationed on the gangway and can sample free the wares of the different merchants before allowing them on board. I also have to shoo off a great number of undesirable and persistent ladies.

A large liner known as the 'Million Dollar ship' is anchored close by in the harbour. She caters for rich people to go pleasure cruising, with a steel magnate paying £5,500 for one suite alone. At night the ship is a blaze of luxury, lighting up the boatloads of hungry women hawking themselves around the cargo boats in the harbour for as little as two liras, about 8d, per woman. It's a funny old world!

Sailing day is bright, which makes all the difference in the world to the Bay of Naples. We pass the sombre and dark old warehouses with gaily painted little brigs moored to the moss-covered quaysides. We alter course to allow for a brig that is entering the harbour under full sail and pass out into the deep and wonderfully clear waters of the bay. A cold wind blows down from the half-circle of snow-capped mountains. We pass strangely shaped lofty islands[viii] with their old castles, forts, and sloping green vineyards; in the distance, the purple forms of Mount Vesuvius and the island of Capri can be seen under their covers of faint white cloud. I am glad to be leaving the vessel at Cardiff; she is not my type with all the red tape, or shall we say 'swank'. A quartermaster sees a good deal when at the wheel – the cringe-making behaviour to the master's face followed by the remarks behind his back when he is not there to hear them. On one occasion, I saw enough at the wheel without even looking at a chart to let the navigators know the ship was on a wrong and highly dangerous course, but I didn't receive one word of thanks. As I said before, the red tape was simply too red. A merchant service officer who, through no fault of his own, is obliged to sign on as a quartermaster is not regarded with much esteem by his so-called brother officers. It is mostly the same in every walk of life; the man without work or money is regarded as a damned nuisance.

It will probably be many years on this vessel before the junior officers attain the rank of captain and some considerable time before the chief officer earns his promotion, but just a fortnight after leaving the liner as a quartermaster, I jump like a rocket straight to my very own command.

13   The Coastal Oil Trade

From a mere quartermaster to a ship's captain in the space of a fortnight is quick going. The letter appointing me as 'Master of our small coasting vessel' arrived one thoroughly wet morning just as I was starting out in a Ford van on what was to be my last furniture removal job – taking our belongings from the cottage by the woods to a house in the town.

Early next morning, tired from my previous long day's work, I survey 'our small coasting vessel' as she lies in the quaint old harbour of Bowling near Glasgow, and am not greatly impressed. With unemployment so rife, I am a lucky man to have such a job, but I'm a little troubled with not having any experience or knowledge of small craft and the coastal trade, which is entirely different from deep sea going. I have been second officer of one of the largest oil carrying steamers in the world and now it looks as if I shall be master of one of the smallest.

The little craft has been a Glasgow Puffer[i] and of late has been carrying whisky up and down the Caledonian Canal. An aging motor barge 65 feet long and 56 register tons, she has been converted to carry about 90 tons of motor spirit. An 80 horsepower Bolinder engine[ii] gives her a speed of six knots in smooth water. Bob, the chief and only engineer, calls her 'the ship-breaker's revenge', but she still floats! There is just room to squeeze into my cabin located under the bridge, a little cubby hole ten feet by four feet with a height of five feet six inches. The engineer, mate, and boy, who will form the rest of the crew, live and cook in the little forecastle inside the almost square bow. I can find no trace of any sanitary arrangements.

I visit the agent's office in Glasgow for instructions and am told to get a crew and to sail at once. They have no idea where I am to sail and have received no orders to advance me any money. I point out that under these circumstances there might be some delay. The whole of the boat, inside and out, is covered in wet paint, it is

Saturday, and I have no charts, no destination, and no money. I leave them to wire the owners and wend my way to a nautical optician to arrange for the repair of the ship's compass, which I had spotted to be in an unhealthy state.

I meet the mate in the Sailors' Home. Old Bill is a big, shabby, round faced and cheery man with a Master's certificate in square-rigged sailing ships and precious little else but debts. He'll take anything, even a job on an oil barge, and is glad of it. Poor old Bill, he may have been a bit wet, but he is a good man and we soon become friendly.

I have now been running around for 30 hours full of importance and with a cold in the head, so I find a bedroom in a country inn and retire with a bottle of whisky for the weekend. By Monday afternoon we are ready to sail. I have my destination – Southampton – some money, and a few charts. The engineer brings on board the joint of beef the landlady of the inn has kindly cooked for us, Bill follows with the remaining stores in a sack, and I, as befitting a shipmaster, come last with the bottled beer and other important instruments.

There's no fuss with leaving the dock, which is very pleasant to one who has been used to big ships. The mate casts off the headline and away we glide down the Clyde like a swan on the water, albeit an elderly black swan. The company wants the oil tanks to be kept dry so we cannot ballast the boat. The trim is bad, deep by the stern and with the whole of the forefoot out of the water. We could very easily drift anywhere with any wind!

Early next morning and in very fine May weather we round the breakwater of Peel in the Isle of Man and make fast under the shadow of the castle. It is impossible to run very far in this little craft without putting in somewhere to replenish the engine cooling water. How different it is coming alongside without the shouting, pilots, and tugboats! As it is Bill's watch below, the boy – Johnny, and a very good lad too – leaves his dishwashing for a moment to scramble onto the quay and make fast our moorings.

There is nobody to welcome our arrival except an aged fisherman who offers to conduct me to the harbour master's office where I can pay the port dues and see about the water. 'Mentioned in *Peveril of the Poke*,[iii] Capt'en,' says the ancient guide pointing a gnarled fist at the castle above us. 'We gotta walk right round the quay and past the Peveril 'otel, Capt'en. They sell the best beer there,' he added hopefully. 'Earl of Warwick[iv] was imprisoned there, no, no, not in the pub, Capt'en, in the castle 'ere. See 'ow the grass is worn away in the grounds, that's the young couples in the summer season, like rabbits they are. Well 'ere's the Peveril. Thanks Capt'en, I could manage to get a pint back, thank yer. There's the 'arbour master sweeping the quay. Good day.'

During the morning we shift the ship into the inner harbour; after an early tea Bill and I stretch our legs along the narrow streets and climb the headland. The moonlight throws strange shadows around the old castle and the incoming tide gurgles softly against our little craft's side. All this seems very strange to me after so many years of deep sea going; if only one could always lie in a peaceful little harbour with romantic castles opposite. However, I have a good deal still to learn about this coasting business.

Next morning a pale yellow sun shines fitfully onto the oily sea as we puff along under the cliffs. It is calm, much too calm. Once clear of the land, down comes the fog as thick as a hedge. Bob cannot spare any compressed air for the ship's whistle and the hand horn doesn't work, but the steady chug-chug of the engine is more effective than either in this silent cold clamminess. The gurgle of the bow wave is the only sound in our world, as if we are sailing into an impenetrable void. The bows can hardly be seen from the bridge despite them being only a short distance apart. With the trim we have it is no use slowing the barge down; she may drift anywhere.

We steer for the Skerries but don't hear their fog signal or that of the South Stack lighthouse later. There is only the wail of a distant ship's whistle on our bow and the grunt of a sailor's horn from somewhere astern. Suddenly a deep bellow comes from right ahead. Bob hurriedly puts some air on our ship's whistle; we give an answering toot, and put the helm hard to port.[v] With a roar close to hand a big steamer passes, totally invisible, leaving our little barge to curtsey to her wash. The wet blanket of fog remains all night and we hear not a sound from the foghorns on Bardsey Island. This seagoing becomes a rotten business!

The engineer cannot remain without sleep indefinitely. Before turning in, he asks me to call him if I hear 'any funny noises' from the now-deserted engine room. And so she chugs along on her own; Bill and I alternate between steering and keeping a lookout, with neither of us having the faintest idea as to where we might be.

In the morning we head in to where we think the land is. The fog suddenly lifts and there, nicely on the port bow, is the Bishop Rock. It is a load off the skipper's shoulders, whether he is of liner, tramp, or barge.

Around midnight under a cloudless sky and full moon the old anchor and some fathoms of condemned crane chain we have for anchor cable go down off the St. Ives breakwater. We need engine cooling water again and Bob, who knows every secluded nook and cranny in the British Isles in which a barge can moor, also has friends here. Mr Lloyd George and the editor of the *Sunday Express* may say that Rio de Janeiro is the most beautiful spot they have ever seen, but they don't have to travel so far. They haven't tried St. Ives on a soft moonlit night.

The breakwater to which we make fast is littered with corks, nets, and lobster pots, and the air is heavy with the scent of our most malodorous industry. The smacks are coming in from their night's fishing. The beach is in an uproar with carts being driven down into the shallow water to bring ashore the morning catch. Standing on an upturned case an auctioneer bellows hoarsely whilst ear-ringed fishermen in their long sea boots and yellow oilskin smocks are busy gutting fish. Rows of cod and ling are spread out on the churned up sandy beach.

'Want a fish, Capt'en?' yells a bewhiskered old salt waving a 14-pound cod about. 'How's this for a bob?' The fish is soon hanging on our forestay.

Facing the beach is the old Sloop Inn. Said to be built of wreck timbers, it reeks of the sea. The house is lined with paintings, a veritable art gallery of Cornish life and scenery. Many well-known artists have lived at this inn. The oak-beamed public bar is crowded with fishermen; it is here I see the gypsy man and his wife I met whilst lorry driving not so long ago. Also here is the champion beer drinker of the British Isles, Jimmy the hanger-on, who will drink a pint of beer and follow it up with 16 more at a sitting if someone else pays for them. A jolly boisterous sea salt-flavoured crowd, they promise me assistance should the weather come on to blow.

Bill, unlike many sailors, will go for a walk as long as the houses of refreshment are not too widely spaced. We climb St. Ives Head from where we can see the golden Porthmeor sands, the distant purple moorland, and our little ship far below, a mere speck against the breakwater. Away to the east is Godrevy beyond the small cargo port of Hayle. You might do a lot worse than take your summer holidays in St. Ives if you are one of those dull people who do not want a casino and a crowd!

I think it was The Golden Fleece[vi] we visited. I remember something of artists, fishermen, gallon jars of ale, and Bill refusing to leave until he had sung some ancient Scottish dirge. On Sunday morning when I take my hat from the top of the stove funnel, the weather is still calm and the sea flushes a rose pink in the rising sun. We plod our way around the lovely coastline with the green bubble of our wake trailing far astern.

This little craft steers far more easily and makes a better course than the electrically geared liner I was steering a few weeks ago. Hand steering it might be, but by sitting back on the bridge rail, it is quite easy and comfortable to steer with one's foot. With our very shallow draught, I suspect we could float after a shower of rain; we keep close in to the rocky coast and the beautiful curves of the bays. It is a very different matter around this part of the coast in a winter's gale; the effects of the waves may suit the artist, but they are far from pleasant to the small coasting vessel.

But now the sea and land are bathed in a mellow heat, the smoke from the forward galley curls lazily up in the still air, and the sound of the church bell comes tinkling across the water. The little barge has averaged seven and one-half knots from Glasgow to Southampton, more than her engine speed, but we have had good tides and the trysail has helped her along. I had understood the boat was wanted urgently, but we have been lying off the oil jetty for a considerable time awaiting orders. As there are no deck stores or gear on board the craft, there is not much work that can be done.

The freshwater cask has to be filled every one or two days which means a long row in the small boat up the creek and then a walk along a lane; fortunately there is an inn at the landing place. To help pass the time away, we take walks through the New Forest with an occasional afternoon siesta on the soft and secluded turf of Beaulieu Abbey. My letters to the office requesting some stores meet with no response.

From the open door of my little cabin I can view the world's largest liners as they pass up and down Southampton water with their wakes causing the barge to bob about. At last we load a cargo of spirit for Eling Creek, a little out-of-the-way place away up beyond Southampton.

I receive a document from the office entitled 'Gas is the enemy of man', and I quite believe it! This literature gives directions on how to avoid the dangers of petrol in bulk, and also the penalties incurred if you do take risks. It says: 'No fires to be lit on board while loading or discharging. No smoking on deck whilst the tank lids are lifted! This is under penalty of instant dismissal.' I can only assume they mean from this world heavenwards. I happen to know the risks well enough, too well for my liking. A friend of mine, a master of a big four-masted barque trading out east and fitted to carry a quantity of oil, was blown up with his ship quite recently.

We must have steam from the shore to pump out the petrol from the barge but the steam hose leaks from end to end so our pump does not work properly. We are obliged to lift our tank lids to put the suction hose from our pump down into the tank in order to pump the petrol into the railway wagons ashore. The boiler, which tries to supply the steam, is situated on the quay but a few yards away from our open tank tops! A seemingly ancient affair, it has a broken spark arrestor, a kind of wire cage over the funnel that should prevent sparks from flying into the air, and the firebox doors must be open for the fire to be lit.

I read through my copy of 'Gas is the enemy of man' a second time – I'm new to all this and I don't want to lose my job! The manager tells me that other ships have discharged here without complaint. It is best to keep in with the manager! 'Gas is the enemy of man' – my hat! With the lack of steam pressure, the discharging is not a success. The manager loses his temper and his last bus home and we return to Southampton with some of the cargo still on board.

I don't want to leave the barge without gaining more experience, but I have no choice when I'm promoted to a larger boat. After a trip or two, I receive further promotion to a larger vessel[vii] yet again, a new oil-fired steamer carrying about 240 tons of spirit.

The vessel looked all right from the distance, but the master's accommodation and the anchor windlass are the only good points about her. I should tell them that the boat is a dud, but there are wheels within wheels and I will merely lose my job.

When she is fully loaded she trims by the head, which means she will hardly steer at all. The little navigation bridge is in line with the top of the funnel so that with the wind anywhere abaft the beam the helmsman is nearly gassed by the fumes from the engine. The vessel is soon found to be leaking all over the place. There are no calibration scales for the oil tanks so it is impossible to calculate the amount of cargo loaded, which makes it rather awkward when I am obliged to sign for a definite tonnage taken on board.

Although almost a stranger to the coastal trade, the actual navigation of the ship is the least of my worries; I lack the experience needed when dealing with the company, a new concern and not yet properly organised. On many occasions I have considerable difficulty in getting the crew's weekly wages. This may sound absurd for a wealthy oil operation; nevertheless it greatly troubles me. I receive the cheque all right, but the difficulty is in getting it cashed.

The traffic manager, who is also in charge of the shipping department, is a shrewd and clever man, better still a gentleman, yet I imagine he has far too much on his plate. I am foolish enough to have the interests of a disorganised enterprise very much in mind and anxious to do my best when I should keep very quiet and feather my own nest, which could so easily be done. I have two great drawbacks to being a success as a shipmaster or, for that matter, to being a success in any business: an inbred distaste for hurting people's feelings, particularly those in an inferior position to myself, and, above all else, a far too sympathetic nature. The world of commerce has a different name for these undoubted handicaps; with the former, you are 'soft' and have no 'push', and with the latter you are 'weak-willed'. I have known cases where a shipmaster has had these peculiarities and got away with them, but only very rarely.

To find a good crew these days is difficult and to keep them is even harder when all you can hear is a continual growl about the state of the vessel. The deckhead of the forecastle, where their accommodation is, leaks like a basket and in bad weather it can't be reached at all from the deckhouse. The petrol tanks start to leak causing all the living accommodation to reek of petrol. The hull leaks badly, with the mate's and engineer's cabins often awash. I am told in no uncertain terms by the party who had bought the ship for the company that any complaints about the vessel are not to go to the office!

The chief officer or mate, whichever sounds the best, is quite a good chap, a Royal Navy Reservist with photography and tennis – whenever he can get a game – as his hobbies. The chief engineer, a Glasgow shovel man with beer in large quantities as his only hobby, is good on the job, which is a difficult one. The two men do not hit it off and one of them has to go. I do the only fair thing and sack the engineer, to my considerable disadvantage though as subsequent engineers let me down badly.

When the beery chief engineer leaves the vessel, the second engineer asks me to recommend him for the job. Being the kindly soul that I am, I think it a good chance for the young fellow, who seems competent, to further his career, but if I were to consider my own interests I should be asking for a more experienced engineer. It is these apparently small good turns one does that can ruin one's own chances of success.

We are the first ship at Poole to use a new depot for the company. It should have been all right, but far from it, for although the tanks and so on are all there, they omit to make a berth for the ship with the result that, at low water, we list over at a dangerous angle and lie yards away from the quay. The mooring posts to make the ship fast have been left inside a high galvanised iron fence surrounding the premises.

Poole is a delightful old port with 19 gentleman's outfitting shops in the main street. The lure of the window displays is such that I end up buying a 40 shilling hand-me-down. There is a sixpenny tram ride from Poole into glorious Bournemouth, with its dirty and paper-littered sands and dozens of wheelchairs with invalids and old people being pushed around the Winter Gardens. Some people actually like Bournemouth!

It is a dangerous practice in an oil-carrying vessel to go to sea with slack cargo tanks. The master should refuse point blank to take a ship to sea unless the tanks are filled up, yet when it is on the direct orders of the company, one has little choice in the matter. It is in this unstable condition that we have our first spell of bad and threatening weather. Although the vessel does pretty well everything except roll right over, we manage to arrive off Shoreham in the dark where we had been told the spirit was urgently required. Then it comes on to blow really hard with almost North Sea suddenness. High tide is around midnight, but no lights into the port are being shown. The sandbar is a smother of foam and the snarl of the shingle too loud to be pleasant. There is nothing for it but to beat back for shelter under the lee of the Isle of Wight.

We anchor off Seaview, a delightful and select little village with narrow old-fashioned twisted streets and steep alleys that plunge straight down into the sea. Charlie and Bill, two ex-Thames bargemen forming my crew, row me ashore. We have been out for the whole of a wet and dirty night and aren't dressed in conventional yachting costume, which causes the other visitors to eye us with what appears to be considerable disfavour as if we are wealthy Americans. It is of no real concern to us; we have to get some stores, and I have to communicate with the office.

It is two days before the gale abates enough for us to return to Shoreham. We find the sea has thrown up a great bank of shingle onto the bar reducing the depth over it at high water from 18 feet to 8 feet. Shoreham is not the easiest of ports to enter on a dark night with a choppy sea. The half-demolished 'Mystery Tower'[viii] is a nuisance in the channel. After anchoring for the night we manage to enter the port on the morning tide with six inches of water to spare under the vessel's bottom. Had the seas not been dead smooth, I wouldn't have tried it.

I know of no place in the world, and that's saying a good deal, to compare with Southwick – the village that faces the locks and canal opposite Shoreham harbour – for the lack of sanitary arrangements to deal with the extraordinary number of dogs that overrun the place. They would not allow it on the front at Hove or Brighton! The state of your boots after a walk around the roads will show you what I mean!

I find it strange that people do not object to an oil depot being built in close vicinity to their dwellings. Perhaps they are unaware of the explosive force of a tank containing 200 or 300 tons of benzol or petrol. They probably think that all precautions have been taken to render living close to an oil depot safe. If this is the case then they are very sadly mistaken and it is, perhaps, a very good thing that they haven't seen what I have regarding these depots and their precautions. The greatest dangers are either from a fire in an adjacent building – a risk that can hardly be avoided – or from sparks from a passing steam lorry and the like. One day there will be trouble.

We have just finished discharging at Thames Haven and are bound for Southampton to load some 63,000 gallons of benzol for Gloucester. If you do not know Thames Haven then you are lucky.

The weather looks fine and it is midsummer. We cast off and get away down the Thames and off Margate, where we can see the young ladies bathing in the sea and, behind them up on the cliff, the North Foreland lighthouse,[ix] one of the oldest lighthouses in England. We round the Longnose Buoy off Margate and head down between the Goodwin Sands and Ramsgate. Steaming close inshore off Deal, we navigate through the Downs where you can see the fine houses in the exclusive St. Margaret's Bay.

We pass close under the lofty chalk cliffs of the South Foreland where the monumental tower[x] built in recognition of the bravery of the wartime Dover Patrol stands beside the lighthouse. In Dover harbour the cross-Channel ferries can be seen lying at their moorings ready to set off like greyhounds on leashes. Now we steer for the low and flat marshland of Dungeness where coasters can shelter in deep water during bad weather on either side of the Ness depending, of course, on the direction of the wind. The Thames pilot cutter is cruising off this point.

We go through the Park, as it is known, in Pagham Bay. There is a safe anchorage off Bognor, which in the time of Henry VIII was deer forest but is now a good place for catching pollock and whiting. Going through the Looe Channel between the Owers shoals and Selsey Bill saves considerable distance, although it is only suitable for small coasters and even then it is as well to know exactly what you are doing.

We cross the entrance to Portsmouth harbour and make fast at the end of a long woodpile jetty extending far out into Southampton water. The pipelines from the shore run along the jetty leaving only a narrow passage for pedestrians, myself included. I have to take a taxi into Hythe and cross to Southampton where I hope the ship's agents will cash the company's cheque for the crew's weekly wages. Never mind the company's regulations that state I am supposed to be on board while the ship is loading, for this is essential!

This performance takes the best part of a day and costs the company £1 for my expenses, in addition to the agent's fees for cashing the cheque. When I write to the company to point out that this time and expense can easily be saved, I am as good as told to mind my own business, so that's that!

With the tide in our favour we are soon down the Solent and off the Needles. Despite the steering being atrocious because we're fully loaded, everything seems to be going well on this voyage, but not for long! The engineer finds that all the engine lubricating oil has leaked from the tank and that we cannot proceed any further. We have to put into Brixham to buy some more oil; we arrive at night, so we have to wait until the following morning before entering the port.

It is a fine sight to see all the Brixham sailing trawlers enter harbour in the early morning. We get underway again and head towards Start Point, which has a ragged coxcomb appearance and can be rounded fairly closely. Land's End is rounded in fine and smooth weather; good for our comfort for one never knows on this vessel what is likely to happen next!

We now head up the Bristol Channel keeping along the Devonshire coast to the foreland, then up through Barry Roads, past Cardiff, and onto Portishead, where we take a pilot to guide us through the dangerous quicksand of the upper Severn.

Once inside the locks at Sharpness[xi], the fat and jovial canal pilot takes the steering of the vessel. Although it is a fine August bank holiday, he not only loses some weight but also most of his joviality before getting the ship to Gloucester. We pass out of the locks into the inner harbour basin.

'Touch ahead, Captain,' orders the pilot.

'Be careful pilot, she's steering very badly.' The pilot puts the helm hard over but she doesn't respond. I have already rung the engines full astern. The mate drops the anchor just in time to prevent the bows from colliding with the stone quay.

'Well, this is about the worst steering son of a female dog I have ever come across,' says the pilot. 'Skipper, we're going to have a lively time on the canal today.'

We pass the busy quays and the big warehouses of Sharpness and make fast to the grassy canal bank to await the railway swing bridge to open after a train has gone thundering across.

'There are 16 narrow swing bridges for the ship to pass through,' says the pilot. 'Seventeen miles in length, this canal, Cap. My two men will walk all the way along the bank to open up the lock gates and to take our ropes as we pass through. I am going to earn my 30 shillings with this packet before the day's out, I can tell you that, Cap.'

The canal passes through some very beautiful countryside with undulating green pastures, golden cornfields, and old farmhouses. The shady banks are lined with willows and angry anglers, all swearing loudly at being disturbed.

'There's a competition going on, Cap, 300 of 'em,' says the pilot.

'Yes, and a swearing competition too.'

'Why don't you load the bloody thing?' yells one sarcastic gentleman. When fully loaded this vessel certainly has the appearance of being in a sinking condition; we have even had vessels signal us in bad weather to ask what was wrong!

At the pretty village of Perton the bridge is lined with waving holidaymakers. The navigation and the distractions become more difficult as we progress further up the canal. The pilot has to dodge small rowing boats manned by shrieking flappers and ensure bathers don't get caught in the propeller. We pass young courting couples and half-naked women taking in the glorious sunshine. Even the pilot borrows the binoculars until he realises we are heading for the bank.

'We're getting near Frampton village now, Cap. If you want some good cider my man will go on ahead and pass it aboard as we go through the locks. Pretty place this, Cap, I live here.'

We make fast to the bank at this straggling village to let a long tow of timber-laden barges go past. The bargees pass the time with the pilot and make a few remarks on the ship's appearance.

Behind the tow comes a little gaily painted barge hustled along by a man on the towpath with a stick and three donkeys moored abreast. The wife combines the duties of helmswoman and a nurse to what looks like her twins. A little further on and around a bend is the Cadburys factory,[xii] probably the cleanest factory in England. Hundreds of milk churns line the quay.

A party of yachtsmen in a large white motor launch can be seen coming towards us, weaving from one side of the canal to the other. The pilot gives a blast on the whistle and ports the helm;[xiii] the helmsman of the yacht waves his hat and starboards his helm right across our bows. To avoid cutting down the launch, the pilot steers our ship straight into the bank. There is an angry tirade between the pilot and a gentleman in a white yachting cap, who dares to suggest that we don't know the 'rules of the road' and says he'll be reporting the incident when he reaches Sharpness. I find this all a bit too much, for no skipper is prepared to have his vessel run down by people such as these. I let them have it through the megaphone good and hard. I have collected a varied and wide vocabulary over the years so I'm able to give them curses in Mexican, Hindi, and Limehouse.[xiv] I hold them spellbound; they bring up bottled beer and settle down to listen before having the impudence to congratulate me on my masterly flow of language.

The canal towpath is mostly on the left bank going towards Gloucester with the brightly painted shacks of the summer campers on the opposite bank. There seems no hurry to open up the old-fashioned bridges; with our terrible steering we are lucky indeed to get through them without an accident. There is a lovely view between the trees of the distant Malvern Hills. As the evening draws on, lovers in what they think are secluded spots grow both in numbers and ardour to such an extent that even the ship's cat and my old sheepdog discreetly turn their heads away from the ship's side.

The overcrowded pleasure steamers are returning from their day trips packed with excursionists yelling like a hoard of wild dervishes. They shave past us, but it seems to me that should we collide there might well be a total disaster.

We arrive safely in Gloucester, a nice old city. We plan to have dinner at the old Bell Inn[xv] with its fine 16th century oak beams, perhaps give the Fleece a visit with its cobbled coaching courtyard before ending up in the Monk's Retreat[xvi] with its cosmopolitan society and electric piano music. We may not have the same good and pleasant voyage homeward bound so for you dear reader, might I suggest you go home by land, perhaps visit Bristol, and from there take a charabanc back to London.

We are on our way home from Gloucester, off the foreland in the Bristol Channel, when the engineer reports it is quite unsafe to proceed any further as the engine is all on the wobble. I turn around and put back to Barry Dock.

The 'marine advisor' to the company comes down, makes an inspection, but can see nothing wrong! He gives us to understand that if, when the vessel is docked and no damage is found, the company will dispense with our services from the master down. This seems rather a strange way of conducting business for no shipmaster in his senses would proceed on a voyage when the main engine is reported to be loose.

The vessel is then hoisted up on a slipway at Penarth. The engine is found to be insecurely fastened to the bedplates and the tailshaft is also out of alignment. With the vessel rolling as she does rounding Land's End, the engine might well have gone clean through the ships side, and I would have been out of a job again.

The riveters on the job tell me they have never seen worse work on a hull; several rivets fall out when they lightly scrape the ship's bottom. The propeller is far too large for the ship. Worse still, a plate from the stern frame protrudes six inches or so lower than the ship's keel so that when the vessel lies aground, as she often must do in these smaller ports, then the whole weight of the ship rests on this plate and the stem so as to strain the vessel very greatly amidships. We do not lose our jobs although we do have three weeks in Penarth, which is punishment enough.

Our next voyage is from Southampton to Maryport, a small port in Cumbria up the Solway Firth. The weather is none too good and it is a long drag from Land's End to the Welsh coast. She rolls so high in the beam sea that no one would be surprised to see the wheelhouse go bodily over the side. It comes on to blow so hard that I shelter in Milford Haven and by Jove, it is a very good thing I do.

As soon as the anchor is down, both the engineers hand in their notice to leave the ship forthwith. Legally they cannot do this, but they were both so seasick on the passage that they are of little or no use; I have to pay them off for our own safety.

There follows a series of extraordinarily severe gales. I have to shift anchorage from Dale roads to off Milford town so I can go ashore and get in touch with the office and ask for new engineers to be sent and also get the company's cheque cashed to pay our wages. The ship's condition has worsened as well. Some rivets must have fallen out from the hull – there is a foot of water washing around the deck of the crew's quarters. The men are fed up and let me know it! The ex-bargemen tell me that had it been anyone other than me as master they would have gone ashore along with the engineers.

The bargemen, the cook, the dog, and I go ashore in our lifeboat. The gale force winds increase to almost hurricane strength and terrible rain blots out the large fleet of steamers now at anchor for shelter in the Haven. This is one of those early gales, almost a cyclone that does all the damage. We try to return to our vessel in the boat, but there's not a chance! A motor boat man refuses £5 to take us, so there's nothing for it but to take shelter in a pub where I make arrangements for us to spend the night. I now have three men and a dog on my hands, and my ship out in the roads straining at her anchor cable with the remains of a crew on board short of food. I retire to a quiet spot in the pub to think things over.

Although still blowing hard the next morning, we manage to return to the ship with the stores. I have to go ashore again to wait for the engineers. No sooner do we get to the beach than it comes on to blow as hard as ever, and again I'm left with three men on my hands.

There seems to be no one remotely resembling an engineer alighting from the late afternoon train at Milford station except a well-dressed and hard-faced elderly gentleman accompanied by a younger man. He turns out to be the chief engineer and, what is more, he has brought a second engineer along with him. After a drink and a yarn a load is lifted from my shoulders for he is a fully certified and experienced chief engineer from Tyneside, and good men from there are generally very good.

At the breakwater the boatman with whom I have previously arranged for a tow back to the ship for £1 claims it is blowing too hard and no longer wants the job.

'Try and get him into the Nelson Arms,[xvii] sometimes a couple of double whiskies works wonders,' suggests the new chief engineer. They certainly do this time, but what with the dog, the luggage, and five men in our lifeboat, only one egg out of two dozen survives the passage.

Maryport docks on a murky night are as black as the pit. In the impenetrable darkness the hand reversing gear of the engine refuses to work and she fails to go astern. The stone quay treats her very rudely, breaking our anchor hawsepipe and badly denting some plates in the bow.

Maryport cannot be called a British beauty spot, with its dirty old warehouses, a ragged wasteland covered in coal dust, the empty wharves, and the idle cranes below a dull Lancashire sky. It is said the railways have killed the coastal trade, even though all the Solway ports are well fitted and easy to access. Cargoes could quite easily be sent to all the smaller ports of Great Britain, but they're not; the docks are more or less deserted.

We set off for home and, in Carnarvon Bay, the wind turns to the north east in a sudden and very heavy squall. Fortunately this is astern of us; with the barometer falling to a surprisingly low level it blows a full gale with very high seas. Having no cargo on board, this little ship is like a balloon on water, rushing on before the gale force winds. The damaged bows and having none too much fuel oil on board prevent me from heaving to. We are not in an enviable position; she makes too much leeway and we cannot bring the sea onto the beam for fear of her probably turning over.

The sleet blurs everything within a hundred yards and the wind howls across the hissing white waste of open water. We are far too close to the Bishop Rock and the dangerous shallow bank nearby. Fighting for every inch of sea room, we're still blown down towards the rocks. The sea is breaking with tremendous force onto the rocks and spray is covering the lighthouse. I'm beginning to think I must try to heave to and take a chance with the bows.

All hands are living in the galley beneath the bridge, which is the only safe place to be, although even that is none too safe right now. The only chart I have for this part of the world is opened out on the cook's seat locker, yet what should have been the coast of Wales is a black oily patch from where the donkeyman has been sitting. Our ship just weathers the Bishop; it is a relief to anchor in the shelter of Dale roads, Milford Haven.

It is all very well for the company to tell me not to dawdle about, but they cannot expect a vessel of only 105 net registered tons to run around Land's End and up the west coast like a penny tram, not in winter anyway. I get away from Milford as soon as possible, a little too soon in fact, for there is a tremendous sea raging off the Longships that makes the turn around the point very risky indeed. The company decides to send the ship to Faversham for repairs to the damaged bow, the leaking accommodation, and the cargo tanks. At the shipyard they say the counter and the stem have never been properly caulked; once this is done, the leaking ceases.

We make a few more voyages to various ports without mishap until we are sent as the first vessel to use the new depot at Rochester. Although it is most difficult to get alongside, both the wharf and depot managers assure me that the berth is quite alright and safe. Something feels wrong but I can't put my finger on it. The manifold to which we must connect our ship's discharge hose is situated in a most ridiculous spot on a little platform underneath the jetty; at high tide a man must stand in water up to the waist to connect the hoses. After much delay and with the help of all hands, the hose is connected and we can commence pumping out the cargo.

I go ashore to the agents with the ship's papers; on my return I find there is something very much the matter. The tide has started falling and the ship is aground with her bows tipped up at an alarming angle. It is quite obvious something is going to happen shortly. We hurriedly disconnect the pipeline and run every mooring rope we have out forward. She tips up more and more until, with a report like that from a starter's gun, all the moorings carry away and she slips off backwards into the river at great speed as if she was being launched from the shipbuilder's stocks. Fortunately, there is nothing coming up the river or there would have been a mess, but as she slips off, the counter of a large vessel moored astern carries away our rigging, the boat deck, and half the bridge. Luckily steam is up and I manage to ring ahead on the telegraph from what is left of the bridge and she is brought up safely.

Although it was impossible for me to know, there is a hard layer of chalk sloping at an angle of 45 degrees or so under several feet of soft level mud alongside the berth. The company doesn't entirely hold me to blame for the incident, but as the ship's master I am responsible for whatever accidents occur on board and I am the one who has to do the explaining.

We take her down to the Spile Buoy, overflow the tanks with seawater to make her more or less gas free, and proceed to Faversham once more for repairs.

I am told the managing director is tired of all these delays and expenses and that they have decided to appoint a new master. Although they put it nicely enough, it means that I, along with everyone else except the engineers, have been sacked. I am sorry indeed to lose the job, but only for the reasons that it is not badly paid and that finding work is just as hard as it has been for a long time. I am glad, however, of no longer having the worry, responsibility, and the risk of being personally liable for taking this wreck of a ship back out to sea. My relief is to be sent to Faversham, so I pack up my troubles in my old sea bag and await my successor.

The newspapers say 32,000 mercantile marine ratings are unemployed and that 2,000 masters and officers will see in the New Year without any hope of finding work. Conditions have never been so bad in the history of British shipping, with master mariners touting for work in the streets of London. It looks as if I shall soon be joining the ranks of the unemployed.

Day after day goes by. I am still waiting with my bag packed but no one comes down except the shipyard manager who is anxious to get the ship away now that the repairs are finished. He tells me that if she isn't taken out of the creek today, the neap tides will prevent her from sailing for a fortnight. He telephones the office, but no one helps him. 'Yes, yes, the Master is here, but he has no orders at all to shift the ship and he says he is waiting to be relieved.'

It is high water and now or never. We cast off with only the mate on deck, leaving the rest of the crew and the dog running frantically along the bank wondering for where we are bound. I tell them to join her at a wharf downriver.

Our arrival off Thames Haven is greeted by three days of dense fog. The manager tells me on the phone to take a cargo of petrol to Keadby, a little village up the River Trent in Lincolnshire, but makes no mention of my relief. We find there is no oil depot yet built in Keadby, so we pump half the cargo into a leaky old barge which then goes up the canal to Sheffield[xviii] to discharge, leaving us to wait for its return for the other half of the cargo.

I'm becoming quite fed up. They say my relief is coming here, but he doesn't show up. It is bitterly cold, my bag is still packed, and I have done more with this ship than many others. I've been a fool unto myself for being too good, so to hell with the ship. I decide to spend some time in the very comfortable village inn where the noise of the rain and sleet hitting the windows is drowned out by the tales of the sailing barge skippers sat at the bar.

There is no chance of being bundled out of this place at 10 p.m. for we take no notice of the landlady, Dora, when she calls for time. We sit in the spacious kitchen in front of the roaring fire. There being, of course, no drinks after hours, we yarn about barges and eat bananas instead!

The familiar outline of the sailing barge has barely changed since the 1860s and can be seen not only on the Thames but also in every out-of-the-way corner of the south and east coasts, and from Ijmuiden to the Channel Islands. They are homely craft with bright streaks of yellow, green, white, and crimson paint and snug cabins and forecastles. I have seen cabins on a Thames barge far and away superior in size and fittings to those of a large modern tramp steamer of several thousand tons.

These barges are rigged in the handiest possible way, which is very necessary with their great sail spread and when the crew consists of only two men, or one man and a boy. They have their work cut out handling the sprit – some are 80 feet long for a 100 ton barge – that runs diagonally across the mainsail; a foresail and jib; sometimes a small spritsail set at the end of the sprit; a large gaff topsail; and the steering of the barge by means of the tiller. The long bowsprit is stowed perpendicularly when not in use. There is not much going aloft for the crew with all the sail shortening being done by brailing, which the barge skippers have brought to a fine art.

I know the skipper of one barge who has made every voyage, except one, on his craft since she was built 20 years ago. The skippers and crews of the barges have a very high reputation as sturdy, independent, good seamen. These men must know the run of the tides, every shoal and sandbank, and exactly when they may take a shortcut across them. You must be a hardy and experienced man to beat up the Thames entrance with a deeply laden barge on a snowy winter's night. Being flat bottomed and drawing as little as three or four feet of water with their leeboards up, the barges can at times make astonishing speeds. With all sails set and a stiff breeze, ten knots is not uncommon. One of the skippers, who is keeping me company in the inn, left Dover in a strong southerly wind in his steel barge carrying 260 tons of cargo and three crew at the same time as we were leaving the Thames, and yet we arrived together in the Humber.

Many hundreds of these barges are leaving the Thames every day; there is said to be 10,000 of them and with them all loaded they would carry over a million tons of cargo. One man I know makes a decent living from owning his own barge. They are often windbound for long periods, though no longer than necessary as the hands are paid on the share system.

My relief, the new master, turns up. He only makes one voyage in the ship back to Southampton before packing his bag and clearing out; one voyage is enough for him. I later heard from the chief engineer that in the six weeks from the time I left her in Keadby, three different masters had been appointed. Not one of them managed to get the ship around Land's End in the winter, and all had to return to Southampton with the cargo still on board. I didn't do so badly after all! No, by God, I didn't, but she did make me nervous!

The shriek of the wind through the quivering stays,
the great green rollers surging by,
the sickening roll from beam to beam,
the low red streak in a cold grey sky.
The icy sting of the flying scud,
the screws mad race as her stern lifts high,
the darkened ports with flying spray,
the lull of the wind like a long drawn sigh.
Rattling pots and pans adrift,
the beat of the engines, all too slow,
as she drifts to loo'ard towards the rocks,
will she weather them? Yes! or No!
The smash of the white-capped seas
that come in great cascades from her drenching bow.
The foaming scuppers, the swaying mast,
the roar of the breakers – Hells own row.
She drifts down closer, God, what a sea,
as she shakes and trembles like a leaf,
and a wall of green leaps up on the beam,
 and throws her round on the boiling reef.
Right under her stem, great jagged rocks,
weird and cruel in the phosphoresce gleam,
That's the worst of fish and chips for supper,
they always make me dream.

Yes, I am becoming so nervous that I had to jump from my bunk to write this down whilst it was in my mind, or perhaps it's too much whisky?

14   THE BULLFIGHT AT INCA

My next venture is as chief officer of a 'monthly' or 'near-trade' boat.[i] This type of vessel goes further afield than the coaster, but the crew have to sign foreign-going articles and find their own food in the same way as on a small coaster. The vessel loads 2,000 tons of patent fuel (a sort of coal brick) at Cardiff for Palma, the port for Mallorca, one of the Balearic Islands.

Outward bound we keep close to the Portuguese and Spanish coasts. The town of Palma is at the head of a deep clear bay and lies at the foot of a semicircle of pine-clad hills. The white stone breakwater is wide and spacious and provides comfortable seating, palm trees, and cafes. In the cool of the evening the population, many of whom are retired British people who have the good sense to live here, slowly promenade its length. One person tells me that the cost of living with rent, servants, and amusements is much cheaper than in England, that the cooking is good and the climate is excellent. What more could you want?

Leading from the main plaza, which is broad and well lit, are narrow and old cobblestoned streets with lofty and heavily shuttered pink and white Spanish-style houses. There are excellent shops and hotels and an immense ancient cathedral, dark and musty inside – a very unusual building. The brilliant yellow trams dash along regardless, rather a nuisance, but there is a non-hurried, restful, and *mañana* air about the place.

Mail boats run daily to Barcelona, quite a short and smooth passage, with about £2 as the first class fare. The big annual bullfight comes over directly from Barcelona and is held in the dull and dusty little town of Inca, which is in the middle of the island about an hour and a half's rail journey from Palma. The train is a rattly and bumpy affair that takes you uphill and down dale on the single line through the heavy red-soiled almond and olive orchards. There are thousands of people and tons of dust on the road from Inca station to the bullring at the top of the hill. The arena is incredibly old with tier upon tier of stone seats, but even the cheapest seats are by no means inexpensive.

The tiers are full to overflowing; the band plays and the crowd roars as the Governor or some such dignitary enters the private box with his party. The ring master, clad in evening dress and mounted on a prancing white horse, leads in the performers who are dressed in many coloured costumes and waving red flags, cloaks, and other garments and utensils. The procession marches around the ring before vanishing to leave two poor mangy-looking horses, each mounted by a heavily padded fellow armed with a long lance, guided by two red-coated attendants.

This is the start of the show. A door opens at the side of the arena and out rushes a sleek black bull. He trots around, has a look at the horses, and then runs off to rub his nose against the stout wooden barrier at the ringside. He doesn't look at all fierce! The howling of the audience seems to bewilder the animal until toreros dance about on horseback in front of him waving a large red sheet.

The picadors, mounted on their old horses, position themselves in front of the now slightly annoyed bull, which, after some considerable deliberation, charges. There is an audible squelch followed by a long and almost human groan as the bull's horns disappear up to the hilt in the side of one of the staggering horses. The picador prods off the bull with his long lance and, while the bull turns his attention to the other trembling horse, the dying animal is led from the arena with its entrails dragging in the sawdust. If possible, the horse's guts will then be pushed back inside its chest and the wound roughly stitched up so as to allow the dying animal to be dragged back into the arena as quickly as possible for the bull to finish him off. First blood having been spilled, the bull becomes angry and charges the other horse, lifting it and its rider high up into the air. The horse falls dead and the padded picador hits the sawdust good and hard with the bull only a foot away from him. The watching toreros head the animal off and the picador walks to behind the wood screens in safety.

 Next into the arena come a gang armed with small darts. I forget what they're called, but it's 'dors' of some sort. Their job seems the most dangerous of all, for the bull is now on the top of his form. The 'dors' let the bull charge and then, like a flash, they step aside as the animal goes thundering past before letting go their darts that stick deep into the animal's sides and hindquarters.

There is a great savage growl from the crowd. More horses are brought on and disposed of by the angry bull, which foams at the mouth and is streaming with blood from the darts, until it appears to me the animal is considerably weakened though still by no means a domestic pet. A picador is injured and then, amidst loud cheers, on comes the matador, the bullfighter himself.

The matador is a cool and leisurely individual who receives a warm reception from both the spectators and the bull. He avoids the animal's fierce charges with a lithe grace that is well worth seeing. He is armed with a long delicate-looking sword and a red cloak with which he plays with the animal. He avoids charge after charge until, panting and shuddering and with lowered horns, the bull paws the sawdust. This is the critical moment; the matador squints along his trusty blade, waiting for the last charge. Then it comes; the steel runs up to the hilt behind the animal's shoulder, penetrating the heart. With a groan and a bellow, the dying animal falls to the ground. I was told the matador must play the bull into a certain position necessary for the kill.

The spectators rise to their feet as one. With howls, hundreds of hats and many flowers are thrown into the arena. Why people should throw their apparently quite good hats about remains for me the puzzle of the afternoon. I cannot, in any case, follow suit, having borrowed the old second mate's straw boater for the occasion. Six bulls and about a score of horses are killed during the afternoon. One matador misses his aim with the sword and is tossed into the air; through some trick of the trade he manages to avoid the actual horns of the bull. The toreros had averted the animal's attention before he can be gored.

The children sitting in front of me seem to enjoy the show. The little ones are just as interested as the little boys at home watching a ghastly murder film at the cinema. I suppose I ought to feel upset at seeing such a grisly spectacle, but how can one be upset when the ladies and the children enjoy it so much?

So selfish is human nature that instead of pitying the poor slaughtered animals, I pity myself. I, like some of the ladies sitting nearby, just wish for a comfortable cushion; the stone seats are as hard as the devil! The women fan themselves continually during the show and seem to be more interested in the other women, and the men, than in the bullfight itself. If I were a horse, I would prefer to be killed almost instantly in a bullfight than to be shipped off amid untold misery to the Continent for sausage meat, as I might be in that wonderfully humane country of England. I've seen both sides of the coin; give me the bullfight every time!

After discharging at Palma, we proceed to a dirty and uninteresting little port near Marseilles and load a cargo of ore for Manchester and Larne. The Gulf of Lyons with its very high seas gives us a sample of the treacherous weather for which it is noted.

The trouble in this vessel is bugs. They swarm all over the accommodation and prevent one from getting a proper rest. I cannot sleep in my bunk and the settee is almost as bad. I've never seen anything quite like it before. The crew are Greek and have been in the ship a long time, which might have had something to do with it.

When the London brewers Messrs Taylor and Walker took over the Swedish Flag public house in Swedenborg Street[ii] and commenced stripping the premises for repairs, the place was so infested with bugs that workmen burned buckets full of these insects. It seems much the same here and, as I have an absolute horror of bugs, I hand in my notice. Besides, there are many other things that I do not like about this ship.

15 LIFE ON A COASTAL TRAMP STEAMER

The British public is best acquainted with large liners and small coastal tramps. Londoners on their river excursions see dozens of these small coastal craft at wharves and under coal chutes. That seedy down-at-heel little vessel with the funnel right aft and the rusty sides can also be seen at many of our seaside resorts. The visitor wandering around the old harbour may well mistakenly view these boats through a halo of spurious romance quite ignorant of the wretched conditions under which the crews of these vessels often live and work. Many do not realise that the discomforts and privations for the men aboard are real enough and that for eight months of the year, when the vessel is at sea, there is rarely a dry patch on the decks.

These craft are the real gypsies of the sea. They roam around the ports of the United Kingdom and the near Continent, often not going to the same place twice for long periods. It is quite surprising the number of different and varied ports these little vessels will visit in the course of a year. Some fine sea boats and some of the most homely ships afloat can be found amongst this type of vessel, but then again one can also find some of the meanest and most squalid of any craft in the British mercantile marine. Some venerable old crocks are over 50 years of age and still going wrong, but somehow they keep more or less afloat. If one keeps the press cuttings of the number of coasting craft lost during a bad winter, the result is surprisingly small. The coaster's cargoes are various in the extreme from bales of footballs to monkey nuts, and from wheat to cattle. Anything and everything is carried, although coal is the mainstay of the coasting business. There is a constant stream of traffic between the coalfields in the west and Ireland, and between the coal ports of Northumberland and Durham to Hull, Grimsby, and the Thames.

Many of these vessels have a crew of only eight or nine persons all told despite them carrying close to 1,000 tons of cargo. The master and one seaman forms one watch on deck with the chief engineer and one trimmer below while the other watch is formed of the mate and the other seaman with the second engineer, who does his own firing, down below. The day man acts as cook and general factotum. This is on the smaller class of boat where a minimum crew is carried; for the better class of coaster, an additional two or three more hands and a cook-steward are on board.

One would imagine the navigation of these small craft to be very much easier than that of the large foreign-going vessel, but this is not the case. One needs far more practice with navigation to be a thoroughly efficient master in coastal waters than to be an efficient deep-sea navigator. The coasting skipper, if he is a conscientious man, will find his mental and physical faculties to be continually on the wrack. His trials and tribulations, both ashore and afloat, would sour the temper of an archangel, unless he is a man very much out of the common. He is his own sea pilot, river pilot, and mud pilot, besides his numerous other duties as a ship's master. As a rule, he will be very ill paid for his labours and responsibilities with around £6 per week being the average wage for coasters up to 1,000 tons, which is the scale I have actually been on myself. Out of this he must pay the steward for his food. He saves the companies far more than this in weekly pilotage fees alone if he is running regularly to a port where pilotage is not compulsory.

The system of navigation in a coaster will be unfamiliar to the deep-sea man until he gets used to it. On the coast there are no bearings, horizontal angles, or measured distances that the deep-sea man employs when in sight of land. The coasting man relies on the compass, the local chart, and the log, but most of all his common sense and the lights, buoys, and the run of the tides that he has carefully memorised.

There is no fuss or red tape about the coaster. I have often been alone at the wheel coming through the Yarmouth roads or taking the ship up the Thames to Gravesend. There is nothing difficult in this, hundreds do it. However, it shows the free and easy methods used in this type of vessel, far too free and easy for safety, because no one should be alone on the bridge in crowded waters. If fog sets in and there are no obstructions between the ship and the shore, the coaster will head slowly towards the land using the hand leadline to establish the water depth before anchoring until the fog clears unless, of course, there is a chance of getting a weekend alongside in port.

I join the first of my small coasting tramps at a small port on the south coast where she is busy discharging flints. Her name was the *Laughing Cavalier* or something along those lines, but I find it to be far from a joke being one of her crew. The last mate had been paid off with delirium tremens and the cabin gives substantial evidence of his addiction.

She is a 'hoodoo' ship, unlucky from the day her keel was laid on the builder's stocks. Ships can be as unfailingly unlucky as human beings; this vessel has rammed piers, tried to knock down stone quays, been in collision, cut down sailing barges and, for a week or two, has been the main object of interest to beach visitors at one of our seaside resorts after running ashore. If she hadn't been a north country strongly built vessel, she would have been broken up a long time ago.

Not only is she an unlucky ship, she is a workhouse for the crew. Getting her ready for sea and securing all her hatch covers after cargo work has been finished is a long and backbreaking job since her gear in such a decrepit state. We sail to Dieppe and load agricultural machinery for London before completing a few trips from the Tyne to London generally loaded with coal, but sometimes with iron girders for reinforced concrete buildings.

Perhaps you will come for a voyage as one of the crew rather than a passenger. You will be more fortunate with your shipmates than is generally the case, for they are Irish, good seamen, and steady. The bosun, an elderly, imperturbable, clay pipe-sucking old seaman, has a better repartee than most Cockney stevedores, which is saying a good deal! He keeps the other two seamen in order; they are all related! When you go ashore with them to buy the stores you will return with something of value to sustain you on the voyage rather than having spent the food money in the pub, as is so often the case.

You will have to live in the grimy hole of the forecastle opposite four quiet and inoffensive Arab firemen who will take little notice of you. You need not worry too much about the work, which can be easily done providing you're not too seasick. Beyond keeping a lookout and hauling on a few ropes when we go alongside the coal chutes, there is little else to be done. If you cannot take your trick at the wheel that is of little matter, for we often find as soon as we get away that there are sailors who cannot steer.

We have a roughish ballast-only passage up the North Sea. Being a light ship, the roll and pitch corkscrew motion is unpleasant even for the most hardened seaman. The forefoot hitting the head seas causes tremendous jars that shake the boat from stem to stern and send the compass spinning round. It is a cold wet morning when we enter Seaham harbour and go alongside a large filthy Greek steamer, which is loading at the coal chutes or 'staithes' as they are locally known. The steamer is

119

hardly visible in the dense pall of coal dust that rises from her holds as 24 tons of the black stuff are loaded every couple of minutes.

At noon she shifts out of the berth to let us into load. Noon is also beer time and I have to go and round up our crew, who have gone ashore to wash off the salt of the sea passage. Stepping ashore, you will not fail to notice the ghastly squalidness of this place, with its dreary drab terraced houses and miserable patches of garbage-heaped waste ground coated with a film of coal dirt. Everything is covered in coal dust except the bar of the public house, which is a relief to find just to get out of the dirt. To my mind there are streets far more sordid along the banks of the Tyne and in other coal ports of the North East than in any waterside slum by the Thames.

On the ship the coal dust penetrates everywhere. We do not like it any more than you would on your dining room table, for even one's expectoration is jet black. We will sail at high tide around 3 a.m. and should finish loading an hour or so before this, which will give the crew time to level off the coal and batten down the hatches ready for sea. This is not a nice job in the wind, rain, and the dark, although it becomes easy enough when it has to be done two or three times a week. As it is, the manual labour on this class of ship has been reduced, through necessity, to a minimum.

Except for an hour or so in the pub I have been on duty since the morning and that is after doing four-hour bridge watches up the North Sea. The mate must attend to the loading of the vessel particularly towards the finish to see she is loaded right down to her marks[i] and no further; at night this is often an acrobatic performance in itself. Besides being on duty all day, I shall also be working the best part of the night, and all for no extra pecuniary benefit. There is no overtime; it is considered to be your job and if you don't like it, there are dozens of men ready to take your place at very short notice. On these coasters, 24 hours' notice on either side can be given and taken.

Just before the sailing time of 3 a.m. you will hear me calling the crew:

'Below there. Come on boys. We're off now.'

'All right, Mr Mate,' is the sleepy reply.

A roar of steam escapes from the pipe behind the funnel, swept away with the wind, for it is a dirty morning. We let go the moorings to the sounds of the jingling telegraph and the rattle of the steering chains.

'Where 'yer takin' 'er to?' bellows a voice as we pass the pier heads.

'London with coal,' yells the skipper through the megaphone, and with a lurch and a roll the deeply laden hull hits the North Sea. She has soon shipped many tons of it on board taking several tons of coal and dust that litter the deck overboard, leaving the foredeck very much cleaner than it had been before.

Now either the captain or I, and two of the crew, will go below for a rest. The watches are set with one man at the wheel and the other putting out the log-line and stoking up the galley fire to make the coffee. With either the mate or the master, who both know the rugged east coast well, on the bridge the vessel moves steadily southwards. Hungry seas sweep the decks fore and aft, the song of the engines goes unfalteringly on, and clouds of black smoke intermittently pour from her skimpy funnel. The white, green, and red lights of passing vessels flit by, and in the engine room below, the Arab fireman maintains a precarious footing for four hours on the stokehold plates. Roasted on one side and cold on the other from where the chill North Sea wind roars down the ventilator onto his bare back, the fireman peers closely into the boiler before raking out the clinkers with a long-handled tool. At the end of the watch after 'cleaning fires', he must come onto deck in the cold morning wind and heave up through one of the ventilators the unburned accumulation of ashes and clinkers from the last four hours. Only then can he wash his tired and dirt-encrusted body before going below to his welcoming bed.

Except a few small jobs around the bridge, there is not much work to be done. The sea has well washed down the rest of the vessel and although the weather has moderated, a wave occasionally comes over the bow and works its way aft. At noon we pass Flamborough Head, the most easterly chalk cliffs of England, where the gulls and seabirds are more common on the north side of the head than the south.

Thirty-six hours after leaving Seaham we are again threading our way through the maze of sandbanks in the Thames before tying up at a wharf near Purfleet. Perhaps tomorrow night we shall once more be bound northwards in ballast for another load. Isn't it an exciting life on these coasters?

On this particular occasion though, our routine is changed. After cleaning out the hold from the dust and coal, a most abominable job, we shift the ship to Jurgens Wharf[i] near the great margarine factory. Here we load a cargo of monkey nuts for Zwijndrecht, a small port near Dordrecht, Holland.

The route takes us from the Schouwen Bank light vessel up the Goeree Gat, a narrow winding waterway that leads us to this small village clustered round another immense Jurgens factory.[iii] After discharging at Zwijndrecht we proceed in ballast through another channel into the River Maas, bound for Amsterdam. The entrance to the canal for Amsterdam is at Ijmuiden, a nice seaside resort. It is a fine wide canal, 31 feet deep, running through flat and fertile-looking agricultural land dotted here and there with windmills, church spires, and isolated 'toy-like' farmhouses. These canals are wonderfully fine methods of transport allowing great long barges that can carry 2,000 tons of merchandise each to move goods all over the Continent.

The ship goes at full speed through what is apparently the centre of the city of Amsterdam, which is said to be divided by canals into 90 different islands. If you have never been to this city you will know just as much as I do about it, and probably more. After our long hours of work, one is too tired to even change into shore-going clothes, let alone go round sightseeing. But I can tell you that the proprietor of the café nearest the ship's berth speaks perfect English, as do many other Dutch people, and he even changes my English sixpence coin for two glasses of good local beer and a packet of Dutch cigarettes.

I wonder where in England a Dutchman could walk into a public house and find good Dutch spoken, and then be able to handover a half-guilder across the bar without any adverse comment? I wonder what he would get in return for his half-guilder even if it were accepted? One cannot help but notice after travelling around these Continental ports that the British can be damnably ignorant when it comes to business.

Early next morning cartloads of timber are brought down to the ship. The crew and I must get the timber on board and rig a kind of trellis some ten feet high along the bulwarks. We load a cargo of 5,000 empty metal drums that weigh a total of only 60 tons. Stowed on deck are 2,000 of these drums, but they are so dangerously high that one cannot see over the top of them properly from the bridge. When going down the canal the helmsman must stand on an upturned box to see ahead; with the weather blowing and raining hard, I find the helmsman to be mostly myself.

This cargo is for Southampton, but it is blowing a south-westerly gale so we shelter off Margate for 24 hours. No sooner are we well in the Channel and off Beachy Head (or 'Suicide Corner' as it is sometimes known) than it starts again. The force of the wind on this floating steel balloon knocks us about all over the place. Many of the drums on deck take flight; being so light, they travel for a good couple of hundred yards in the air before hitting the water. If the trellis and the lashings hadn't been so good, we would have lost the whole of the deck load. As soon as the ship docks in Southampton there is a mad scramble ashore to get something to eat; we have been right out of food for 24 hours.

From here, we make a voyage in ballast up the North Sea to Middlesbrough. It is a strange sight going up the Tees at night; it looks like the Hell we were told about as boys and to where we would be sent when we were naughty. It is not an easy port to enter for a nervous skipper doing his own pilotage; the flares from the huge blast furnaces at the steelworks can be blinding. We load iron girders for London, but then there is no more business and the ship is laid up.

Everyone on board is paid off and I am unemployed once more.

After a month or so of idleness, I am lucky enough to get a berth as mate of a vessel trading regularly between London and the Continent with general cargo. What a treat it is to carry decent clean cargoes again rather than coal. When one's home is in London this kind of seagoing is the most satisfactory for one can predict, within 12 hours, when one will be home again. Everyone settles down to an orderly and well-planned routine.

Showing how casual the treatment of seamen is, the National Maritime Board[iv] make a ruling without the slightest warning that everyone's wages shall be reduced by ten shillings a week. This is rather a drastic reduction when the wages can't be considered to be high in the first place. It now means that my pay is down to the bare subsistence level for a married man. I have heard, however, that smuggling tobacco and other goods across from the Continent to the Thames can make some good money. It's quite easy on these coasters to land the stuff before the customs officers arrive on board providing the proper arrangements have been made beforehand. I don't have to say that only dishonest persons would do this kind of thing, or do I?

This job in the regular trade, along with my luck, is too good to last and a few months later the ship is laid up and the crew paid off. How sick can one get of this casual employment!

One gets to know the Thames quite well on this trade. From where the charm of the good old River Thames originates is a difficult question to answer, but there is no river quite like it in any part of the world. There is certainly nothing beautiful about its lower reaches, even up as far as London Bridge, and it has none of the beauty of the upper reaches of the Elbe before Hamburg. The Seine is infinitely more beautiful and yet there is something about the Thames; its very dinginess perhaps, or might it be because we're homeward bound?

Sitting back in what appears to be my permanent invalid's deck chair in the grounds of the hospital and lucky to still be sitting in that, I close my eyes and can see the ship heading up the river as vividly as if I was on her only yesterday.

We enter the river via the Prince's Channel at the Tongue lightship and pass between Margate, the Tongue, and Kentish flat sands to the south and the Longsand, Shingles, and Girdler sands to the north. Lying to the north of the Nore lightship are the Maplin Sands, a vast area that practically reaches, though under different names, from Hole Haven to the River Crouch. Like everything else, one gets used to picking out the particular channel buoys from what would seem to the layman to be an utterly confusing conglomeration of lights; it certainly does require constant practice before one can be completely at ease in these channels. Clearing the old pile Chapman lighthouse, we steam past Canvey Island before reaching petrol-smelling Thames Haven, where many huge oil tankers are moored alongside the berths. We round Lower Hope Point opposite the Mucking Flats and steam along Lower Hope Reach before arriving at our destination of Gravesend.

On these coasting vessels one becomes acquainted with many of the wharves and jetties on the Thames from close to London Bridge to Greenwich – if you find yourself with some time to spare, the little-known museum here is interesting and well worth a visit – and then right on down to Tilbury. Each of these places has their memories to the coasting man of their advantages, disadvantages, and peculiarities. Something good or bad has happened to you or your ship at every one of them, like difficulty in getting ashore over the mud and climbing the high perpendicular ladders at Bellamy's Wharf[v] at low water, or the long tramp to get a drink or stores when tied up to some obscure jetty at West Thurrock. I think back to the busy Free Trade Wharf;[vi] being caught in the neap tides for days at the bottle wharf at Charlton; the solid mass of barges in the Regents Canal Dock; negotiating the many gates and turnings to enter some of the Surrey and Commercial docks; and the bleak, forbidding bitter winter's morning spent hoisting the old chain moorings from the river bottom to make the ship fast at Cherry Garden Pier,[vii] Rotherhithe. The quaint old public houses where the back rooms overhang the river at high water can tell many a queer tale of the Hanover Hole Tier,[viii] the Woolwich buoys, Bow Creek, Purfleet, and so on. I shall never see any of them again; perhaps it might have been as well for me if I'd never seen them in the first place!

And then there are the upper reaches[ix] of the river, which can be very beautiful in summertime. I know quite a bit about some of them after spending a summer through to midwinter looking after a yacht that was tied up to the bank close to a well-known 'gay' riverside hotel.[x] This was at a time when finding an officer's berth in the mercantile marine was almost impossible. The owner of the boat, a London manufacturer and a very nice man, only visited the yacht once a week and never slept on board, giving me plenty of time to not only observe the river in all its moods, but also the people on it in a good many of theirs!

It would be as well if people understood that when they light the lamp at night in their green canvas-covered punt they are giving a free shadow show that the lonely man on the yacht cannot help but see, things that they might have wished to be kept a little more private. Yes, I saw quite a lot of riverside and hotel life!

After the first month or so, I got my meals at the hotel with the staff. The dinner alone for visitors was 15 shillings, but my meals out the back were costing me 12 shillings a week. Hotel life behind the scenes may be interesting though not edifying. The hotel was described as 'a picturesque spot with ideal surroundings, where the landscape lends enchantment to the eye - the sound of rippling water harmonising so sweetly with the distant music, and all around is beautiful.'

In 'the magnificently illuminated grounds' were elderly city men walking with their young daughters, or at least I suppose they were related because they seemed very fond of one another and didn't like being by themselves in the moonlight.

It was a beauty spot all right with the gaily painted houseboats and their lady occupants, lovely girls drifting past in punts, noisy beer-drinking excursion parties, and horrid, vulgar people – how I wished to be with them as I leaned over the yacht's side and watched them pass by. Puffing grimy tugs and barges occasionally penetrated these reaches.

Everything shut down with the onset of winter and the fog. The chestnuts from the trees overhanging the yacht fell like bombs onto her quiet decks day and night. The brown angry river roared past in full flood and the nearby bungalows were submerged. I had to row my dinghy across the tennis lawns to the hotel steps to get my meals. In the hotel, the cellars and kitchens were flooded and I had to walk several hundred yards in water up to my knees to get ashore, and that was after rowing to where the riverbank should have been.

As I mentioned before, the run from London to the Continent comes to a full stop, and I find myself looking after two laid up vessels in the Tyne. I am being paid the sum of £2 per week[xi] as a watchman with which I have to find my own food and support my wife and three children living at the other end of the country. This may sound all right to you, but they could get a dozen men to hang about these ships for even less money. With row upon row of laid up ships in the River Tyne, many of which have their late captains as watchmen, this job is the best I can do for the moment, perhaps for a long time!

My ships lie in a tier off North Shields, which means I have to scull ashore for all the stores and my letters. I am allowing an out-of-work shipmaster to sleep on one ship; he is a family man with no dole, no money, no prospect of a job, and cannot even go before the mast because of an internal injury received in the war for which, of course, being only a mercantile marine officer, he receives no pension. On board the vessel on which I live, we have a kind of communal stewpot. There are many tons of bunker coal on board so I can keep a roaring fire going in the galley night and day. At times we have no food at all and I have to tell the butchers in Shields that a large Alsatian has been left on my hands on the ship so they could sell me a whole lot of bones for the stewpot. Around these ships is an epidemic of financial cramp with attacks of the 'give me or lend me' symptoms being very prevalent.

I work hard on that boat and with the help of the children of the chief officer of another boat in the tier I paint the decks and the funnel and varnish all the wood in the living accommodation. How those boys revel in the paint and the ghastly mess they sometimes make, but we do a whole lot of work that could never have been done while the ship was running. I receive no thanks or extra pay for all this – quite the reverse in fact – and shall always be extremely sorry I ever started maintaining this vessel. There is no need for me to do this work, which doesn't fall under the duties of a watchman at all. As it is, I have the greatest difficulty for some weeks in getting the poor wages they paid.

My friend, the unemployed master, makes some very clever toys based on a round bit of painted wood that pricks your finger with two hidden needles as soon as it is picked up. He wants me to go round the pubs with him to try to sell these masterpieces. I decline his proposition; some people might not see the joke although they will feel it!

Then there is the idea of singing and playing the banjo in the street. One turn of that is quite enough particularly when you can do neither properly and it makes you feel a perfect ass (until, I suppose, one gets used to it).

Fortunately, another job turns up sooner than expected as a mate of a boat running between Ghent and Strood, a little place close to Rochester, with cargoes of manure. The route to Ghent is up the Schelde River about 14 miles beyond Flushing, through the canal locks at Terneuzen, and then along about 20 miles of deep water canal with its banks lined with avenues of trees.

At the moment a pound note goes a long way in Belgium, and because beer is cheap in Ghent, everyone who drinks, and that is everyone in the ships I have been on, goes on the spree without fail. I should think the row of 'sailor's' cafés does well. It is the usual custom, of course, to ask the girls to have a drink, but here, before you know where you are, they have collected the whole family from grandpa to baby to share in the gratis refreshment.

Quayside thieves abound in Ghent, as they do in most Belgian ports. It is as well to lock yourself in your cabin at night and to keep the porthole closed as these people have brought this form of robbery to a fine art.

The vessel now makes a few voyages to various Continental ports and London. We take a cargo to Bremerhaven before going through that very splendid piece of engineering work, the Kiel Canal.[xii] The canal is not only lit up as bright as day at night, it is also wonderfully clean and orderly. There is no silly humbug here about the pilots; every vessel, whatever her size, must take one. We are bound for Rostock, a pretty little port in the Mecklenburger Bucht in the South Baltic.

The Germans seem most genial; one would certainly not think there had been a war! Perhaps they are after our English cigarettes, which are greatly in demand. We load a cargo of wheat for London, yet on completion of discharge, the ship is laid up and another job is gone. I'm not a ratepayer in the Fenchurch Street district so I'll not be helping to wear out the pavement looking around the shipping offices.

I get a job as third mate on a large new tramp steamer[xiii] bound for South America, but the wages as third mate for a married man are at starvation level. In normal times I should not be sailing as third mate, but after the coasting life this deep sea job is just a rest cure. I have only nine hours' duty in the 24 instead of working all day plus the hours of a nightclub waiter on top. It is indeed a real rest, although the voyage can hardly be called a pleasant one, with the captain on the booze and being a man of dangerous temper, and also the most misanthropic navigator that ever sailed the main.

This does not worry me, however, and the man leaves me alone. As far as officers go he is rather up against it, for all three of us are a bit hard boiled ourselves! The food is very poor, just three different names for meals, and for supper a mug of cocoa and what appears to be a few safety razor blades the steward calls cheese!

All the officers leave upon the ship's return to the Continent. Although she is a new British-built vessel, she is a cheap one that isn't entirely seaworthy. The Board of Trade surveyors could not have surveyed her very well. I could stay and have the second mate's berth, but I leave her anyway. She is lost with all hands shortly afterwards, not at all to our surprise.

16   THE SCOTCH COASTER

Next in my mad pursuit for wealth I go as mate of what is the meanest and most sordid of any class of vessel in the British mercantile marine: a Scottish coaster. I join her along with a little Cockney cook-steward at a wharf in the lower reaches of the Thames. When hearing of the job, I rush to join without having any idea as to what type of craft she might be or, indeed, what wages will be paid. As the ship is just finishing discharging and waiting for a mate and a cook before she can sail, we are known as 'Pier Head Jumps'.

On the platform of the riverside station an old person approaches us, his bristling white whiskers as black as his greasy dungarees.

'Are ye the gentlemen for the *Lilywhite*?' he asks.

'We are,' I reply.

'Weal, ye can get aboard, yon's the wee craftie. For a saxpence the porter will put your gear…' The porter says he won't do anything of the sort after he eyes my huge sea bag.

'That's all right,' I say, 'we're away for a bite to eat, then we'll take a cab.'

'Ah weal mon, dinna be ower long, we sail soon.'

The old chap turns out to be the skipper despite the cook-steward thinking he should be in a home with his old age pension rather than going to sea. He is a Highlander and without exception the hardiest man I have ever come across. Over 75 years old, he never wears an overcoat even in the coldest and wettest of weathers. He is a mean and narrow-minded old man, a non-smoker, a non-drinker, and too old to be safe as master of such a ship, but a very courageous person both morally and physically. He must have had extraordinary strength as a young man.

The vessel itself is about the dirtiest and most dangerously neglected steamer I have ever clapped eyes upon. The ancient peeling paintwork fails to hide the mass of rust she has become; one of the masts is as rotten as an overripe pear with most of the ratlines[i] carried away and not renewed; the fairleads[ii] for the mooring ropes appear as if they might come bodily away from the deck; and the bridge rails are hardly safe to lean against.

The vessel was laid up for two years until quite recently. Her engines overhauled, she was being sent back to sea to make hay while the sun shone by earning money during the coal strike.[iii] She carries about 900 tons of cargo but everything has been cut back in the name of economy. A month's stores would fit into an empty soap box and the navigational gear consists of a few out-of-date blueback charts,[iv] a tiny pair of warped parallel rulers, some broken dividers, and a barometer always pointing to 'very dry'. There's not even a ship's clock. Fortunately, the compass, the hull, and the windlass are good; the accommodation is very roomy and dirty. My bunk is an old Italian Renaissance model, the faded colour of which is repeated in the soft green silk bunk curtains which blend harmoniously with the dingy yellow of the once white paint. A novel touch is added to the deck above my head where a square of peach-coloured satin canvas has been nailed to keep a leak from dripping onto my bedding. I must have the colour scheme altered; we are so particular on these coasters!

There is no wheelhouse and the ship's wheel manually turns the rudder except when in very narrow channels when the steam is turned on to give assistance to the helmsman. Neither lifeboat can be swung out because of a timber construction to hold spare bunker coal is in the way, and the dinghy leaks hopelessly. The port sidelight, most needed of all, hardly shows a light through some fault in the burner. The decks leak and several securing cleats are missing from the hatch coamings. There are only two worn-out threadbare tarpaulins on each hatch, and no spare ones. Her being a very wet vessel, the matter of hatch coverings is of the utmost importance.

Britannia rules the waves and so she ought when they can get men to take such a contraption to sea for lower wages than those fixed by the National Maritime Board as is the case, I now understand, with most Glasgow-owned coasting vessels. What a farce it is! Had I known all this, I would not have joined her at all, and had I not been a family man, one voyage would have been more than enough. The last two mates made only one voyage in her and they were both married men. I do not exaggerate one bit about the condition of this vessel and yet one hears a lot about the Board of Trade surveyors examining ships. They must have passed this one, yet she is unquestionably another unseaworthy craft I have been unlucky enough to find.

The crew consists of the old skipper, a doddering old Irish bosun, an out-of-work miner they have picked up from somewhere who is quite useless as a sailor, myself, and a burly jolly Irishman in my watch. Below, there are the chief and second engineers, both ex-firemen, and four of the 'Bright Young People' from the slums of Glasgow to do the firing.

So this floating mass of coal dust and rust casts off, bound for Hamburg. On a fine Saturday afternoon she puffs her way up the pretty upper reaches of the Elbe, past the districts of Blankenese and Altona with their country mansions, dainty yachts, camping parties, and bathers. Below Altona is Hamburg's Margate with a strip of sand, hundreds of bathers, boat hirers, and bands playing. Germany caters for the masses far better than any other country to which I've visited.

Twenty steamers, nearly all colliers, are coming up with the tide. Hamburg has never experienced anything like this demand in handling export coal before, yet they deal with it in a wonderfully efficient manner. Every east coast collier seems to be here. There are vessels from every part of the British Isles waiting in tiers to be loaded with coal, all because of this ridiculous strike:

> I cannot understand this coal strike. What can the leaders of the affair be thinking? They must have known, even a man that gets his living out of a Trade Union must have known at once, that as the Mercantile Marine carry this foreign coal, and the trimmers will discharge it, that the strike is hopeless. If we had refused to carry any of this foreign coal then the miners would have won without delay – the thing is utterly simple, so that there is only one conclusion, and that is some very dirty work going on – somebody making money, I do not mean the shipowners, they always do make money out of the country's troubles, as they did in the war, and again now, I mean Trades Union heads are feathering their nests and it is useless on the face of what I have said to deny it.
>
> If the mining industry is really so hard hit as is made out, why is there no fund for the for distressed mine OWNERS as well as miners, better still a fund to relieve the colliery shareholders, there is some very real distress amongst those, people ruined far more than the actual miners themselves, and we never hear anything of this.

The ship goes under the coal tips at Altona at once and in an hour is blacker than ever. The loading continues throughout the night. It is far too warm to sleep in the cabins below with the portholes closed; every two minutes a truck of coal roars down the chute that is within a yard of my head when I'm in my bunk, so I go for a blow to a beer garden a little further down the river.

The old skipper cannot rest. On my return to the ship he is arguing with the coal trimmers, who cannot understand a word of English, let alone Scots!

'Mon, ye must trim up to yon bulkhead a wee bittie,' the old man shouts at the quite uninterested trimmers, 'aye mon, they dinna ken a word o' the English language.'

There is dense fog all across the North Sea on the homeward passage. Suddenly the fog bank lifts slightly and above it a crane can be seen on a cliff.

'We are no so bad,' says the skipper, 'we're off Aberdeen.' That is where years of coasting experience comes in – just one glance at a cliff above the fog and the old man knows exactly where he is.

The weather kindly clears for us to pick up the red-banded lighthouse at Buchan Ness, three miles south of Peterhead. We have to pass through the entrance of the convict-built breakwater[v] into the outer harbour before reaching the inner one. This harbour consists of winding twisted quays separated from the grey North Sea by a granite seawall overhung with brown ozone-smelling nets that are guarded by rows of large white gulls. The air is as bracing as champagne, but I don't think it is ever warm in Peterhead, a cold and hard little fishing town.

During the week the streets are deserted, but on Friday nights and Saturdays, the fishing fleet blocks the harbour like sardines in a tin, and all is bustling. Motor lorries rush and bump along the dock road that is crowded with long-booted fishermen in blue jerseys and gutting girls in their oilskin skirts and gaily coloured sweaters. Overhead the big gulls whirl and scream. The ice cream carts are busy amongst the drifters, although hot rum would seem more appropriate to me. On Saturday nights the streets and the pubs are full. There is a little museum here, a credit to the town that contains some interesting relics of the whaling days for which the port was once noted. Some of the rustic arches in the gardens of the solid granite built houses are formed from whalebones. The gaol is a grim-looking building; when a ship has cargo for the breakwater or the prison the convicts are sometimes put aboard to discharge it.

Only a week after leaving Peterhead, we have already been to Hamburg for more coal and are back, this time to Dundee. The town, in which the last witch in Scotland was burned at the stake,[vi] has the reputation of being a rough spot; no doubt it was so in the old whaling days. Now it seems very mild and well-ordered with Woolworths being the main attraction despite the music hall, where Sir Harry

Lauder[vii] is performing, being just over the way. Here we can get rid of the miner, who has been trying to act as a sailor, because it is his home port. Had he been sacked and we were in another port, then his fare home would have had to be paid by the shipowner.

We are bound for Hamburg again. The old skipper lays out the course with the help of his walking stick, while I hold down the springy and sticky old chart. He digs vaguely at the chart with the broken dividers, unable to see because he has misplaced his spectacles. I tell him the course he has put on the chart passes north of Heligoland.

'That's naething to speak of mon, bide a wee bitie 'till I get ma stick straight.'

Mrs Besant says in the theosophical magazine: 'The point from which you start decides the direction you shall follow if you seek some special goal.'

We find the mouth of the Elbe. Considering everything, this ship makes some remarkably good landfalls. On this run we have to dodge the fishing fleets. There are a thousand miles of nets spread nightly in the North Sea during the herring season and millions of herrings have been landed in Yarmouth in a single day.

What a vessel this is! With only the Irish sailor and me on deck, we are approaching Cuxhaven where we have to show a blue light to change the pilot. There isn't a blue light on board so the sailor makes a flare with paraffin-soaked waste lashed to a deck scraper, creating a flare that lights up half of Germany. Even the pilot has to laugh when the engine room telegraph goes wrong a little later.

It is blowing a great gale when we're homeward bound once more, this time with coal for Aberdeen. We anchor weather-bound close to the vast expanse of sand that separates the entrance of the Elbe from the Weser. The tide runs with great strength on the ebb, bending the spar buoys back to the water level. Under the angry sky at low water, the vast stretch of uncovered sand is shades of grey and brown and is desolate in the extreme. The moaning winds against the incoming tide cause a tumbling sea. There is something infinitely lonely and sad about these stretches of tidal sands and mud banks that to all outward appearances have no attraction, and yet hold a very peculiar and strong fascination to people with a similar nature to mine.

A steamer nearby drags her anchor and comes down on top of us, her counter actually bobbing up and down over our bulwarks. She misses smashing our bridge by inches before finally drifting clear. The old captain decides to get underway when the weather improves a bit, but he is a little too impatient. As soon as we clear the river, she meets heavy seas and is reduced to no more than a walking pace with the precious bunker coal being used to no purpose. It is weather seldom experienced at this time of the year, with the decks being swept by waves from end to end.

Our berth in Aberdeen is right up in the town in an area surrounded by pubs. Even the very coal carts that are backed down to the quayside to receive our cargo appear clean – in Aberdeen! A very nice city indeed with many attractions with this ship as one of them owing, I suppose, to the notice in the local press of our very rough passage. Many visitors come down to look at the vessel, but until my new flannel trousers arrive from home, I don't look to be a particularly impressive chief officer. My knees are nearly through the ones I'm wearing, but I have put on a collar in honour of the City of Aberdeen; the place is well worth it.

From here we sail to Bremen and load coal for Glasgow. The drink is cheap in these Continental ports, which suits our firemen. I don't think I have ever seen people quite like them before. Some of the steel from the shipyards must have been bred in them for their style of living would very soon kill an ordinary man. They are drunk all the time, blindo in port and sodden with it at sea. I'm no mother's darling myself having seen the effects of drink in all parts of the world. I've been mixed up with drink and drunkards it seems for years, but these people are different, the real 'Red Biddy'[viii] drinking boys. It is incredible how low human beings can sink.

I have read many speeches on the subject of drink and drunkards by Church of England bishops, social reformers, and temperance lecturers, but what would they say about the firemen on this ship? They would say a lot of utter nonsense for the simple reason that they know nothing at all about the subject, although they think they do! These firemen are of some use in the world because they are working, and that is of the greatest importance to this country, although it must be admitted that their hard work is, to some extent, keeping them alive by throwing off the effects of the drink.

The best of our Police Court Missionaries[ix] are poor men financially, yet they come as near to following the teachings of Jesus Christ as is possible in this country, and to understanding these people when they are not actually living and drinking with them. The Police Court Missionary sees life very much in the raw at times, as do we on this class of ship from Glasgow.

Personally I'm not against the drinking, although I must say I like it in pleasant surroundings with a certain amount of decency, but there is neither here. I don't think I'm so much of a snob, but I cannot get used to seeing the engineers come straight from the engine room to sit down for their meals covered in grease and sweat only to eat their food with their hands without even washing them. At least the chief engineer eats his kipper with only one hand!

If we had been born and bred in the slums of Glasgow we might easily be very much worse than these firemen. It is said that drink is a curse; we are all under a curse of some sort. Business is the curse of the capitalist, poverty and insecurity the curse of the manual working class, work the curse of the drinking classes, dreaming the curse of the artistic class, snobbery and narrow-minded ignorance the curse of the middle class, pomposity of the clerical class, and so on, and so on.

We pick up the land at Duncansby Head[x] and with the strong westbound tide the old packet canters along between the Caithness shore and the island of Stroma. The tides in the Pentland Firth[xi] run more strongly than in any other part of the British Isles.

In the terrific gales that occur around here a few times every year, everything seems as if it is covered in thick smoke. Seas striking the rocky coast throw foam hundreds of feet into the air and the roar of the surf can be heard 20 miles away. On the north shoal the breakers rise to 60 feet, increased by the uneven nature of the bottom and the tides of great velocity. Today all is fine, but in the eddies off Stroma the sea appears rough and it takes two of us at the wheel to manually steer the ship.

The only time I ever see the old skipper animated in the slightest degree is when he points out the beauty spots of his native land. 'Yon,' he says, pointing to a queer-shaped pinnacle of rock of the same nature as that off Heligoland and old Harry in Poole Bay, 'that's the Old Man of Hoy,[xii] Kitchener[xiii] was lost round about there. Aye mon, it's a bonny country, look at yon gran mountains,' he continues, waving at some sad-looking hummocks in the direction of Cape Wrath.

We plod on past the entrance to Loch Torridon, with some wonderful cloud effects after showers of almost tropical-like rain, and into the Inner Sound. It is indeed grand and wild country. Whales often get caught in the shoal water around the Sound of Harris and seals can be seen in October in the quiet and unfrequented lochs. We pass through the Narrows of Kyle and the little village of Bagh Strathrie[xiv] where the island mail boats lie moored at the quay at the foot of the sheep-dotted and sweet-smelling moorland. In the month of August it is light enough to read on the bridge throughout the night.

Entering the Sound of Sleat we see a smart sailing yacht anchored off a strip of golden sand with a shepherd's cottage close by. I notice Lady Eastham, charming as usual, drinking a cocktail whilst pacing the deck dressed in salt-stained galoshes.

She is evidently none too pleased at seeing this ghastly monstrosity of ours rushing past at full speed. Further down the Sound, I spot Lord Drinkwater with his yachting cap on board his elegant yawl drinking a whisky and soda. You may think it a little odd that these society people are doing these strange things, but according to 'Dragoman' of *The Daily Express*, royalty are doing just the same. He wrote: 'the infanta Beatrix drank orangeade in a chinchilla and grey fox coat at the reception and, moreover, she held the orangeade in her hand.' A difficult job, we ordinary people prefer a glass!

There seem to be no trees in these parts and it's quite cold. No wonder society visits the area to cool off after Cowes and Goodwood. The waterfalls and braes sparkle like diamonds in the sun and the mountains tumble down sheer to the water's edge so that we could moor this vessel alongside the cliffs. A noticeable feature in these western highlands is the intense whiteness of the lighthouses and cottages.

We have a bit of a sea run to get round Ardnamurchan Point, past Tobermory, and into the beautiful Sound of Mull with the white town of Oban right ahead. Seeing the Craignure Inn with its motor ferry and the nearby old castle stronghold[xv] and the big estates, I have to give credit to the rich Jews and the shipowners for selecting such a lovely spot in which to live in summer.

We meander through the narrow channels into the Sound of Jura. Our skipper knows every foot of the way, as anyone coming through here at night must do with a large vessel. As dusk is falling, we nearly run down a sailing craft without any lights.

'A local boat, I dinna doubt,' says the skipper.

'Yes,' I reply, 'she must have been because she wasn't wasting any paraffin!'

The River Clyde is remarkably empty of shipping with the vast shipbuilding yard of John Brown's, a town in itself, strangely still. We find Cardiff to be just the same with no ships in the port and grass growing under the once rarely still coal hoists. Things are very much not as they should be.

We now make a few trips between Rouen, Antwerp, and London. English is more universally spoken in Antwerp than in any other Continental port. The cathedral and the usual sights are well known. Less well known is the fact that one may buy for a penny at some dockside cafes a plate of hot cooked winkles as large as oysters, and that the outskirts of the docks are very unsafe places to be alone at night. Very unsafe indeed!

Once more we go to Hamburg and load coal for Hull, but it never gets there!

It is blowing hard enough when we sail, and at noon the next day off the Borkhum we are caught in a north-westerly gale and increasingly steep and dangerous seas.

I have never seen the North Sea looking so really ugly. Tom, the Irish sailor cum fisherman in my watch, also does not like the look of it and suggests we ought to have put back into port a long time ago. Seeing the old tarpaulins covering the hatches, and knowing that if she does ship a good one it will be the last thing she will do, I call the skipper to give him my views.

'Mon, look at yon bunker coal we shall have wasted, but I'm no saying it dinna look verra bad. Wheal, wheal, let's get her round.'

But that is easier said than done. We manage to get the helm hard down and she begins to turn when the six-foot wheel takes charge and whizzes back, throwing both Tom and me onto the deck. It nearly breaks the sailor's leg and takes all the use from my arm for some time, but with the three of us we eventually get her round and on the course back for Heligoland. It is just as well we do for the gale increases to hurricane force and we are lucky to get into the mouth of the Elbe and anchor with a long scope of cable more or less under the lee of the sands at Neuwerk.

Just after midnight with Tom and myself on watch, I am feeling very tired and cold and sit for a few moments on the chart room settee.

'Mr Bones, Mr Bones.[xvi] Lookout, Christ!' I hear Tom yell. I rush out on deck to see a large steamer not a stone's throw away, bearing right for us amidships. She is light and totally unmanageable in the hurricane. By a miracle of good luck the wind edges her off slightly so that she collides only with our bow, which she smashes up pretty thoroughly. Away goes our anchor, the cable roaring out of the hawse pipe with sparks flying. The great shadowy hull of the other vessel fades away into the darkness and sleet. Fortunately the engineer is ready when I ring full ahead on the telegraph to prevent us bearing down onto the ship lying at anchor astern of us.

We head up the river in the terrific winds and intense darkness not knowing whether we are sinking or not. If we had been cut down amidships nothing could have saved us that night, and yet when Tom and I meet in the galley a little later we roar with laughter!

The old skipper seems a bit dazed but takes the wheel while I go forward to find the extent of the damage. The stem and the anchors have gone altogether; the forepeak tank is full, although the bulkhead seems to be holding. We steam slowly up the river and wander about off Cuxhaven trying, without success, to get a pilot. No notice is taken of our flares until it is seen that we shall soon be in a dangerous position on the shifting sands with a falling tide, and only then does a pilot come out to take us into the harbour.